THE 30-MINUTE SHAKESPEARE
ANTHOLOGY
18 STUDENT SCENES WITH MONOLOGUES

"Nick Newlin's work as a teaching artist for Folger Education during the past thirteen years has provided students, regardless of their experience with Shakespeare or being on stage, a unique opportunity to tread the boards at the Folger Theatre. Working with students to edit Shakespeare's plays for performance at the annual Folger Shakespeare Festivals has enabled students to gain new insights into the Bard's plays, build their skills of comprehension and critical reading, and just plain have fun working collaboratively with their peers.

Folger Education promotes performance-based teaching of Shakespeare's plays, providing students with an interactive approach to Shakespeare's plays in which they participate in a close reading of the text through intellectual, physical, and vocal engagement. Newlin's *The 30-Minute Shakespeare* series is an invaluable resource for teachers of Shakespeare, and for all who are interested in performing the plays."

ROBERT YOUNG, PH.D.
DIRECTOR OF EDUCATION
FOLGER SHAKESPEARE LIBRARY

The 30-Minute Shakespeare Anthology
978-1-935550-37-2
Adaptation, essays, and notes © 2015 Nick Newlin

There is no royalty for performing scenes or monologues from *The 30-Minute Shakespeare Anthology*. Ebook editions are available in all standard formats, and a downloadable PDF edition is available at www.30MinuteShakespeare.com.

Cover design by Sarah Juckniess
Printed in the United States of America

Distributed by Consortium Book Sales & Distribution
www.cbsd.com

NICOLO WHIMSEY PRESS
www.30MinuteShakespeare.com

Art Director: Sarah Juckniess
Managing Editors: Katherine Little, Leah Gordon

THE 30-MINUTE SHAKESPEARE
ANTHOLOGY

Based on the plays of
WILLIAM SHAKESPEARE

Abridged AND Edited
by NICK NEWLIN

Nicolo Whimsey
Press

Brandywine, MD

To the memory
of my uncle
Peter H. Sellers
a true Renaissance man

Special thanks to Joanne Flynn, Bill Newlin, Eliza Newlin Carney, William and Louisa Newlin, Michael Tolaydo, Hilary Kacser, Sarah Juckniess, Katherine Little, Eva Zimmerman, Leah Gordon, Tanya Tolchin, Frank Harris, Julie Schaper and all of Consortium, Leo Bowman and the students, faculty, and staff at Banneker Academic High School, Charlie Feeser, Paul Reisman, Robert Young Ph.D., Peggy O'Brien Ph.D., and the Folger Shakespeare Library, especially the wonderful Education Department.

✳ TABLE OF CONTENTS

✳ INTRODUCTION

There is something about a Shakespearean monologue that sets it apart from all other speeches. It is not just the iambic pentameter, although no other playwright uses that structure with such brilliance. It is the way the language transports us into the inner life of the speaker, using words so descriptive and colorful as to almost magically bring characters into existence, fully human and breathtakingly dramatic.

This collection contains nine monologues for male characters and nine for female characters. You can act across gender lines, of course. Shakespeare would approve, since male actors generally played the female roles in his time. I saw a wonderful all-male production of *Twelfth Night* on Broadway in 2014. Female high school students originally performed many of the male characters' speeches in this book on an Elizabethan stage as part of Folger Education's annual Secondary School Shakespeare Festival in Washington, D.C.

If you are reciting the monologues for an audition, unless you have a reason for doing otherwise, you may prefer to stick to roles that correspond with your gender. The choice is yours. In some of these monologues, a female character is disguising herself as a male. The dramatic and comedic possibilities for gender bending already exist in the plays—have fun!

This book is designed for students, teachers, and anyone interested in furthering a love for Shakespeare's poetic language, characters, and stories. It is perfect for a classroom, audition, competition, or performance. Everyone from middle and high school to graduate school and the professional world will benefit from this collection of scenes with featured monologues, all of which I have directed in performance with groups of high school English students at Folger Education's Secondary School Shakespeare Festival.

Some of these speeches are famous, recognizable as part of Shakespeare's greatest hits. For freshness and discovery, I have also picked several monologues that are less widely performed. They are all are gems. I hope you and your audiences find the same beauty and drama I experienced when studying and presenting the pieces on stage with young actors.

The Monologue Notes that accompany each speech are designed to provide suggestions on choices you can make to bring the speech to life. Always begin by examining the text closely and determining what the words mean, both literally and in the context of the character's story. Be sure to decide what they mean to you personally as well. With Shakespeare, we always return to a close reading of the text. Enjoy this process of discovery. Unlocking the magic of Shakespeare's words leads to a powerful dramatic experience for actor and audience. The choices you make in a monologue are always yours alone, but the text is your ultimate guide. Speak the words with understanding, nuance, dynamics, coloring, and emotion, and the result will be a moving theatrical experience.

I have placed the monologues within the context of a scene from each of the eighteen plays in *The 30-Minute Shakespeare* series; the monologue appears in a different font. Thus you have two (or more) options. You can perform the scene with a group as part of a classroom activity, performance, or competition, or you can extract the monologue from the scene and perform it solo.

You will enrich your understanding of the speech by exploring it within the scene, experiencing how others in the drama affect your role. Nobody lives in a vacuum. Shakespeare's characters exist in relation to each other. Even if you do not perform the scene with other actors, I suggest that in addition to delving into that particular scene, you read, or preferably watch (or act), the whole play. This will allow you to become even more familiar with your part and deliver your speech with awareness and authority. I've included recommended videos of great performances for each monologue in this collection.

I list the scenes and monologues here by play, scene, number and gender breakdown of actors, monologue character, monologue gender, theme, and number of lines in the speech. Most monologues are one to two minutes long, and the scenes average about five minutes. Three of the scenes (*Love's Labor's Lost*, *The Merchant of Venice*, and *The Tempest*) are between eight and ten minutes in length. Even the shorter speeches are so rich in linguistic beauty and dramatic power that the work you do in bringing them alive will be time well spent.

SCENES AND MONOLOGUES AT A GLANCE

All scenes approximately five minutes in length unless otherwise specified. All monologues approximately 1–2 minutes in length.

AS YOU LIKE IT: ACT II, SCENES I AND VII
Four male characters; possible narrator and non-speaking roles
MONOLOGUE CHARACTER: *Duke Senior, male*
MONOLOGUE THEME: *the uses of adversity*
17 lines

THE COMEDY OF ERRORS: ACT II, SCENE II
Two female characters and two male characters; possible narrator
MONOLOGUE CHARACTER: *Adriana, female*
MONOLOGUE THEME: *the inseparability of lovers and the contagion of adultery*
37 lines

HAMLET: ACT III, SCENE I
One male character and one female character; possible narrator
MONOLOGUE CHARACTER: *Ophelia, female*
MONOLOGUE THEME: *"a noble mind o'erthrown"*
12 lines

HENRY IV, PART 1: ACT III, SCENE II
Two male characters; possible narrator
> MONOLOGUE CHARACTER: *Prince Henry, male*
> MONOLOGUE THEME: *duty and redemption*
> *22 lines*

JULIUS CAESAR: ACT II, SCENE I
Four male characters and one female character; possible narrator
and non-speaking roles
> MONOLOGUE CHARACTER: *Portia, female*
> MONOLOGUE THEME: *sharing secrets with your spouse*
> *26 lines*

KING LEAR: ACT III, SCENE IV
Five male characters; possible narrator
> MONOLOGUE CHARACTER: *King Lear, male*
> MONOLOGUE THEME: *physical and mental tempests*
> *18 lines*

LOVE'S LABOR'S LOST: ACT V, SCENE II
SCENE LENGTH: 8-10 minutes
Four female characters, and five male characters; possible narrator
> MONOLOGUE CHARACTER: *Princess, female*
> MONOLOGUE THEME: *austerity and patience for love*
> *25 lines*

MACBETH: ACT I, SCENE V; ACT II, SCENES I AND II
One male character and one female character; possible narrator
> MONOLOGUE CHARACTER: *Lady Macbeth, female*
> MONOLOGUE THEME: *ambition*
> *16 lines*

THE MERCHANT OF VENICE: ACT IV, SCENE I
SCENE LENGTH: 8-10 minutes
Five male characters and two female characters (disguised as men); possible
narrator and non-speaking roles
> MONOLOGUE CHARACTER: *Portia, female (disguised as Balthazar, male)*
> MONOLOGUE THEME: *"the quality of mercy"*
> *23 lines*

THE MERRY WIVES OF WINDSOR: ACT V, SCENE V
Six male actors and three female actors; possible narrator and non-speaking roles
>MONOLOGUE CHARACTER: *Falstaff, male*
>MONOLOGUE THEME: *"love, which makes a beast a man, and a man a beast"*
>*16 lines*

A MIDSUMMER NIGHT'S DREAM: ACT IV, SCENE I
Six male characters and four female characters; possible narrator
>MONOLOGUE CHARACTER: *Oberon, male*
>MONOLOGUE THEME: *retracting cruelty for love's sake*
>*30 lines*

MUCH ADO ABOUT NOTHING: ACT II, SCENE III
Four male characters; possible narrator
>MONOLOGUE CHARACTER: *Benedick, male*
>MONOLOGUE THEME: *giving up the argument against love*
>*27 lines*

OTHELLO: ACT II, SCENE III
Four male characters; possible narrator and non-speaking roles
>MONOLOGUE CHARACTER: *Iago, male*
>MONOLOGUE THEME: *making evil out of good*
>*27 lines*

ROMEO AND JULIET: ACT III, SCENE V
Two male characters and three female characters; possible narrator
>MONOLOGUE CHARACTER: *Nurse, female*
>MONOLOGUE THEME: *settling for a practical husband*
>*14 lines*

THE TAMING OF THE SHREW: ACT V, SCENE II
Five male characters and three female characters; possible narrator and non-speaking roles
>MONOLOGUE CHARACTER: *Katherine, female*
>MONOLOGUE THEME: *what a woman owes her husband*
>*44 lines*

THE TEMPEST: ACT V, SCENE I
SCENE LENGTH: 8-10 minutes
Nine male characters and two female characters; possible narrator and non-speaking roles
    MONOLOGUE CHARACTER: *Prospero, male*
    MONOLOGUE THEME: *The virtue of forgiveness*
    27 lines

TWELFTH NIGHT: ACT II, SCENE IV
Three male characters and one female character; possible narrator
    MONOLOGUE CHARACTER: *Viola, female (disguised as Cesario, male)*
    MONOLOGUE THEME: *how women love*
    15 lines

THE TWO GENTLEMEN OF VERONA: ACT II, SCENE IV
Two male characters and one female character; possible narrator
    MONOLOGUE CHARACTER: *Proteus, male*
    MONOLOGUE THEME: *a new lover's image pushes out a present lover*
    23 lines

PERFORMING MONOLOGUES

START ORGANICALLY

I recommend reading the speech silently and then reading it aloud to yourself. After you do this, read it out loud again, maybe experimenting with dynamics such as softening your voice when you feel the text calls for it and then speaking louder and with greater emphasis when the spirit moves you. Listen to how the words sound. How do the words feel physically and emotionally as you speak them?

Don't worry initially about what everything in the text means. Just speak the words and be curious as to what your character is saying, how she feels, and what story she is telling. That is what I mean by "start organically." Don't rush to the dictionary, the notes to the play, or a video of the performance. Researching a role is an important part of the process, but I recommend you start with your own unique curiosity. You are the one who will be bringing himself to the role, so start alone.

STUDY THE TEXT

Next, look more carefully at the words on the page. Print out your monologue and pick up a pencil. (You can find easily editable copies of Shakespeare's plays at www.folgerdigitaltexts.com.) Circle the words you have questions about. If you don't know what a word means, take a guess based on its sound or appearance. Look at its context. Based on other lines that your character speaks, what might it mean? Then look it up in the dictionary. See if its etymology, or origin, comes from another word. Be curious! Each word is a piece of the puzzle that is a Shakespearean speech.

I recommend the notes to the Folger Shakespeare Library editions of the plays. They are informative and insightful. In addition to providing definitions of what these words meant in Shakespeare's time, they also explain the longer historical, literary, mythological, and religious references that Shakespeare uses. The more time you spend studying the minutia of the text, the better your stage interpretation will be. It's exciting work because you know that everything you learn, you can then put into your performance!

STUDY PERFORMANCES

There are numerous recordings of Shakespeare's plays readily available for viewing. Whether on YouTube, PBS, cable or satellite TV, streaming sites, or apps, the twenty-first century has provided us a wealth of astounding Shakespeare performances. Use the resources available to you, and study how great actors have rendered your monologue. Study the bad ones, too! Figure out what works for you and what doesn't.

It is extremely important to watch **more than one** rendition. You don't want to parrot somebody else's performance. Shakespeare has been performed so many different ways that you can access a wealth of different interpretations to inform your work. At the end of each Monologue Notes, I have included suggested films and recordings to watch, and there are many others at your fingertips. If you have an opportunity to see an actual live performance of a Shakespeare play at some point, so much the better! Videos are great tools, but there is no substitute for experiencing a live performance of a Shakespeare play, whether by students, amateurs, or professionals.

THE TEXT

WORDS AND PHRASES

Throughout the Monologue Notes, I refer to "coloring" words. When you speak a word, try to imbue it with the emotion or attitude of the speaker. Some words lend themselves more to coloring than others. Pick particularly evocative words and do not gloss over them. Great Shakespearean actors milk the sound of the words for all they are worth. A properly colored word can hang in the air like a painted masterpiece and give richness to the text and your performance. There are numerous example of this in the Monologue Notes.

Aside from choosing words to color, you must choose key words to **emphasize**. Study a Shakespearean actor's performance. You will notice that in any given line, there is a word or phrase that is stressed. It is given more punch than other words in the sentence. Experiment by reciting your lines out loud, emphasizing a different word or phrase until you arrive at your own portrayal. Just one change in emphasis can alter the meaning or tone of a speech.

RHYTHM

Many of the monologues in this collection are written in iambic pentameter. Make sure you know which monologues feature this rhythm:

> *But mercy is above this sceptered sway.*
> *It is enthronèd in the hearts of kings*
> (Portia from *The Merchant of Venice*, Act IV, Scene I)

Often when a line is one beat longer, for example, it presents an opportunity for you as an actor to capitalize on that change by adjusting your delivery. I learned from my colleague Michael Tolaydo, Professor of Theatre, Film, and Media Studies at St. Mary's College of Maryland, that the iambic pentameter rhythm is like a heartbeat: ba-**bum** ba-**bum** ba-**bum** ba-**bum** ba-**bum**. When the iambic pentameter structure is disrupted, perhaps the character's heart skips a beat, and he has an emotional reaction that informs the speech. Look into the rhythm carefully, and when it varies, see if you need to change with it.

Feel the iambic pentameter, but do not fall into the habit of stopping your words at the end of each line. Speak them as sentences, naturally. This can be a challenge with longer lines since you may run out of breath before the end of a passage. Carry the vocal energy to the end of the sentence. To do this, you will have to find beats in the text.

BEATS

A "beat" is a pause in your speech. Proper use of beats can turn an ordinary monologue performance into a great one. Not only does the "beat" allow the actor to present a dynamic speech, but it also gives your character the opportunity to process the words and absorb them internally before moving on to the next phrase. Give the audience a chance to watch your character think and respond emotionally to what she is saying. A well-placed beat gives the speech shape and nuance. Go through your monologue with a pencil and draw a line wherever you want a beat. When you observe other performances, notice where the actor pauses. Just as in great music, the silence between the words in a Shakespeare monologue can speak volumes.

PERFORMANCE

TURNING POINTS

A great monologue has a beginning, middle, and end. As the actor, you must determine where the turning points are. The Monologue Notes in this book will help you identify these moments. You might discover instances where the mood shifts and the character takes on a new attitude or makes a new discovery. Perhaps the first part of the monologue is a question, and the second part is an answer. Maybe the mood moves from hate to love or from despair to hope. Study the text and watch performances, then experiment on your own to see if you can unearth a turning point to give your speech a dramatic arc. Your character undergoes a change in the speech, and you will want the audience to see this.

MOVEMENT

Movements and gestures in a monologue should not be forced. At the same time, you cannot speak your monologue completely still (unless the text calls for it, of course). The best movements are motivated by the text and can range from a simple hand gesture to a tumble, a leap, or a fall. The scenes in this collection have stage directions written into them. These are meant to be starting points or suggestions to get you moving. Your own movements will evolve as you begin to take ownership of your character's words.

The more you study your character by mining the text for clues and studying others' performances, the clearer a picture you will gain of how your character walks, stands, speaks, sits, and moves on the stage. If a movement or stage direction feels odd to you, try something different. Develop a physical vocabulary that is economical and expressive. You do not need to move on every word or phrase, but you do need to decide how to physically illustrate your words.

TRY IT ANOTHER WAY

Somewhere in the rehearsal process you will find an interpretation of your character and speech that works for you, and you will be performance-ready. Until that time, feel free to experiment. Try the speech softly, then loudly. If you have recited the words with great tragic emotion, then try the monologue as a comedy just to shake things up. Vary your word emphases, beats, word colorings, and movements. There are always alternate interpretations of any speech. Allow yourself at least one different way to play a speech, sentence, phrase, or word before arriving at your definitive version. You won't know what interpretation works best for you until you have tried a number of possibilities.

BRING YOURSELF INTO IT

How do you make a Shakespeare monologue or character your own? You have read the text carefully, studied film or stage versions, and experimented with delivering the speech in different ways. The won derful thing about your role as an actor is that there is only one of you. Nobody can perform Shakespeare like you can.

Does anything about the speech make you feel something emotionally? We hope that it does, but if it is leaving you unmoved, use your imagination. If you had lost a brother and missed him terribly, how would you feel? We all feel love, jealousy, confusion, excitement, joy, anger, and sadness. We have all lost something (or someone) and missed them. If you are lucky enough never to have experienced the same tragedy as your character, try to sympathize with her plight and identify a time when you felt a similar emotion.

If you don't feel anything, then simply let the text do the talking for you. These monologues are full of beautiful, expressive phrases. Give them their due. Shakespeare's words possess a magic of their own that touches people's hearts and awakens their imaginations. Trust the words. Express them with as much care and artistry as you can. The work you put into preparing to perform a Shakespeare play will reap its rewards. Shakespeare has a tale to tell, and you are the one to tell it.

✳ AS YOU LIKE IT

CHARACTERS IN THE PLAY

The following is a list of characters that appear in this scene of As You Like It.

DUKE SENIOR: Living in banishment

AMIENS
JAQUES | Lords attending on the banished Duke

ORLANDO: Son of Sir Rowland de Boys

ADDITIONAL LORDS IN FOREST

NARRATOR

SET AND PROP LIST

SET PIECES:
Tall stool with burlap or paper covering to look like short tree
Short stool with burlap or paper covering to look like tree stump

PROPS:
Leaves
Rock for Duke Senior
Packs for forest dwellers
Bread and fruit to put in packs
Sword for Orlando

✳ *AS YOU LIKE IT:*
ACT II, SCENES I AND VII

The Forest of Arden.

SOUND OPERATOR *plays* Sound Cue #1 ("Forest music").

Enter **NARRATOR** *from stage rear, coming downstage left.*

As **NARRATOR** *introduces the roles, players enter from designated sides of the stage, cross in character, and exit the opposite side of the stage.*

NARRATOR
> In the Forest of Arden, Duke Senior and his exiled
> lords make the best of their life in the woods, where
> they meet Orlando, who himself has been cast out
> by his older brother Oliver.

Exit **NARRATOR** *stage left.*

SOUND OPERATOR *plays* Sound Cue #2 ("Forest music").

Enter **DUKE SENIOR**, **AMIENS**, *and two or three* **LORDS**,
like foresters.

DUKE SENIOR
> Now, my co-mates and brothers in exile,
> Hath not old custom made this life more sweet
> Than that of painted pomp? Are not these woods
> More free from peril than the envious court?
> Here feel we not the penalty of Adam,

The seasons' difference, as the icy fang
And churlish chiding of the winter's wind,
Which when it bites and blows upon my body
Even till I shrink with cold, I smile and say
"This is no flattery. These are counselors
That feelingly persuade me what I am."
Sweet are the uses of adversity,
Which, like the toad, ugly and venomous,
Wears yet a precious jewel in his head.
And this our life, exempt from public haunt,
Finds tongues in trees, books in the running brooks,
Sermons in stones, and good in everything

AMIENS *(admiringly)*
Happy is your grace,
That can translate the stubbornness of fortune
Into so quiet and so sweet a style.

They sit down to eat, pulling out fruit and bread from their packs.

Enter JAQUES from stage left.

DUKE SENIOR
Why, how now, Monsieur Jaques! *(surprised at*
JAQUES'S *happy demeanor)*
What, you look merrily!

JAQUES
A fool, a fool! I met a fool i' the forest,
A motley fool; *(begins to prance about merrily,*
then stops sadly) a miserable world!
(drops to his knees) O that I were a fool!
(kneels and faces AMIENS, desperate to make his point)
I must have liberty as the wind,
To blow on whom I please; for so fools have; *(blows*

on **AMIENS,** *who holds his nose and recoils)*
But who comes here? *(stands and backs up a few
paces to observe)*

Enter **ORLANDO** *from stage left, in a slight panic, sword drawn.*

ORLANDO
Forbear, and eat no more.

JAQUES *(noticing that the others have food and he doesn't)*
Why, I have eat none yet.

DUKE SENIOR *(polite but cautious)*
What would you have?

ORLANDO *(still threatening)*
I almost die for food; and let me have it.

DUKE SENIOR *(graciously gesturing)*
Sit down and feed, and welcome to our table.

ORLANDO
Speak you so gently? *(humbly on one knee, bows)*
Pardon me, I pray you:
I thought that all things had been savage here;
(sincerely and sadly) If ever you have look'd on
better days,
If ever from your eyelids wiped a tear
Let gentleness my strong enforcement be:
In the which hope I blush, and hide my sword.
(puts his sword back in sheath)

DUKE SENIOR
True is it that we have seen better days.

ORLANDO
> Then but forbear your food a little while,
> Whiles, like a doe, I go to find my fawn.

Exit ORLANDO *stage right.*

DUKE SENIOR *(to* JAQUES*)*
> Thou seest we are not all alone unhappy:
> This wide and universal theatre
> Presents more woeful pageants than the scene
> Wherein we play in.

JAQUES *(pauses)*
> All the world's a stage,
> And all the men and women merely players:
> > *(walks stage right)*
> They have their exits and their entrances;
> And one man in his time plays many parts,
> Last scene of all,
> That ends this strange eventful history,
> Is second childishness and mere oblivion,
> Sans teeth, sans eyes, sans taste, sans everything.
> > *(long pause while the men absorb this image)*

DUKE SENIOR *(realizing the mood has dropped, to* AMIENS*)*
> Give us some music; and, good cousin, sing.

ALL *(sung as they exit)*
> Blow, blow, thou winter wind.
> Thou art not so unkind
> As man's ingratitude;
> Thy tooth is not so keen,
> Because thou art not seen,
> Although thy breath be rude.
> Heigh-ho! Sing, heigh-ho! Unto the green holly:
> Most friendship is feigning, most loving mere folly:

Then, heigh-ho, the holly!
This life is most jolly.
Heigh-ho!

Exit ALL *stage right.*

✳ AS YOU LIKE IT: PERFORMANCE NOTES

I directed this version of *As You Like It* with a group of ninth graders in 1999. The play is ideal for beginner actors, as it allows them to enter a romantic new world full of colorful characters and beguiling language.

These stagings do not require elaborate set pieces, and music (played on a boom box in this production) can set the tone quite well. If a cast member can play a classical instrumental snippet live, then so much the better. I am continually impressed with the power of music to set a mood.

Use simple staging to introduce characters and illustrate major plot points. This theatrical device underscores my belief that in order for audiences to "get" Shakespeare, they must first "get" the story. This version of *As You Like It* uses music and tableaux to bring viewers into the world of the play. Careful blocking is a good tool for illustrating plot and character as well as eliciting emotion from performers. Novice actors often hold back on their responses, not wishing to embarrass themselves. When the body illustrates an extreme emotion it is sometimes easier for the voice and facial expressions to follow suit. Tableaux are an effective rehearsal tool, useful for exploring simple visual statements that illustrate the text, clarify plot points, and illuminate relationships.

In this production of *As You Like It*, the young actor playing Duke Senior had a strong physical presence and a powerful voice, and he had a knack for emphasizing certain words to achieve maximum effect. Actors should be encouraged to experiment with which words (or syllables) to stress in a speech, since changes in emphasis can elicit varying meanings. This shows players that how the words are spoken greatly affects their meaning and interpretation.

Simple costume and prop choices help actors color their roles. Duke Senior had a cape that he threw over his shoulder dramatically before striding off stage. If an actor has skills or training in dance or other disciplines, try to incorporate them into the play. The best ideas and pieces of stage business often come directly from the actors and their unique talents.

Look for staging patterns that can be repeated to give rhythms to a production, like motifs in a piece of music. As with other aspects of speech and movement, physical distance between characters on stage speaks volumes about their relationship. By combining Shakespeare's great language with our actors' minds, bodies, and spirits, we create together a living, breathing work of art on stage.

AS YOU LIKE IT: ACT II, SCENES I AND VII

This excerpt (Act II, Scenes I and VII) is set in a forest, so prerecorded bird whistles provide a nice acoustic scene setting. There are two stools covered in brown wrapping paper to look like stumps, and a few leaves and stones scattered about the stage complete the set dressing. There is something satisfying about a minimalist approach to scenic design. It allows actors and audience to fill in the picture with Shakespeare's words and their imagination. My experience has been shaped by nineteen years of participation in a student festival; eight schools a day tread the boards at the Folger Library, leaving little time for elaborate scenery.

If your situation differs, and you have the resources and inclination to spend more time on scenic design, this too can be satisfying, especially if there are members of your group who can contribute creatively. I prefer a scaled-down approach, but I acknowledge my own tastes and the uniqueness of my venue. I encourage you to explore every aspect of the spectacle that will enhance your theatrical experience. I do urge directors to continually return to Shakespeare's rich text as their primary dramatic source.

On the line "sermons in stones," Duke Senior picks up a stone, puts it to his ear like a seashell, and passes it on to the other group members, who likewise raise it to their ears to listen. The final actor shrugs and places the stone back down on the stage. When Jaques enters, he gives Senior a special forest handshake (of the actor's invention). On Jaques's famous "Seven Ages of Man" speech, he puts his hand on each of his three seated comrades' shoulders during each of his final three phrases: "Sans teeth (first comrade), sans eyes (second comrade), sans taste (third comrade), sans everything (Jaques alone)." These characters are "brothers in exile," so it is nice to have some group sequences to illustrate their unity. This staging serves to reiterate the inclusive nature of the speech. This journey from birth to death is one we all share. After "sans everything," all four men bow their heads in silence, which gets a laugh.

The fine line between comedy and tragedy fascinates me. That unison head bowing could just as easily have resulted in a thoughtful moment of silence from the audience as they absorbed the fact of our own mortality, but this adolescent audience chose laughter as a response. The key is for the actors to play it straight. Perhaps the sincerity of their somber physical response to Jaques's speech was what tickled the audience's funny bone. Regarding the timing of the speech, it is important to pause after "sans everything." It is during that pause that the players solemnly digest Jaques's weighty words, and where the laughter has a chance to emerge. When blocking this scene I did not predict audience laughter, but I was happy it occurred. There are other moments (such as Juliet's death in *Romeo and Juliet*) that do not invite laughter, and if it occurs, we must study the cause to prevent it in the future. Likewise, when audiences grace us with their laughter, we should try to replicate the circumstances. It is not an exact science but it is worthy of study! Make sure to have at least one rehearsal in front of an audience to gauge potential responses.

When Orlando enters and encounters the exiled lords, his fear and bravado stand in contrast to the mellowness of the peacefully snacking forest-dwellers. This is a funny moment because the contrast between Orlando and the foresters is evident in their body language. Whereas Orlando spins about suspiciously and brandishes his sword, the forest men gnaw languidly on their food and pay him no mind.

This scene in our performance ended on a rousing note, with the band of foresters clapping out a rhythm and Jaques lagging behind the rest, busting out a few unique and personal dance moves. Personality cannot be taught, but providing a rehearsal environment of experimentation and fun can encourage its expression. After each verse, the entire group shouts out a loud "Heigh ho!" and they exit the stage with a loud and simultaneous cry of "This life is most jolly!"

✳ *AS YOU LIKE IT:* MONOLOGUE NOTES

ACT II, SCENE I: DUKE SENIOR MONOLOGUE

I selected this monologue because it spoke to me. What does this mean? When something "speaks" to you, it resonates emotionally; it touches a nerve in you. It makes you feel something. If you have a choice when choosing your monologue, pick something that makes an impression on you, either emotionally, intellectually, or aesthetically—or all three! If the monologue is assigned to you (i.e., you did not choose it yourself), try hard to find something in the words that has an emotional impact on you. Always start with the words, and then extrapolate to the character, the plot, and the play as a whole.

In this speech, the phrase that has the greatest emotional impact on me is: "Sweet are the uses of adversity." This could be considered the main point, or the centerpiece phrase, of the monologue. All the words before and after this phrase are essentially extrapolating on one idea: Hardship has a sweet purpose. Think back to times in your life when you encountered difficulties or misfortune. Was it all bad? Or did the experience lead to something better or provide a lesson? See if you can personalize Duke Senior's words based on your own feelings or memories.

If you have not experienced hardship's "sweet" side, then dive into Duke Senior's words and see if you can conjure up the feelings in the words. Even if you do not feel any emotion yourself, perhaps by giving the words their emotional expression, the audience will feel something!

I looked up "adversity" in the dictionary and found the following: Origin Middle English: from Old French *adversite,* from Latin *adversitas,* from *advertere 'turn toward.'* Sometimes researching the etymology, or origin, of a word can lead you to an interesting interpretation. In this case, I imagine Duke Senior turning toward a cold wind and relishing, rather than cowering from, its bite on his face.

The first two sentences of the monologue are in the form of questions. Duke Senior is asking his "brothers in exile" whether the woods are not sweeter than the "envious court." Here we can color contrasting words and give warmth to words like "co-mates," "brothers," "old custom," "life," and "sweet." How do you "give warmth" to words? The voice is expressive: If you stretch the vowels a little and soften the consonants, the word "brother" sounds soft and welcoming. If by contrast you speak with a more choppy and clipped tone, you can similarly color the words that describe court life with a colder sound. You can speak the words "painted pomp," "peril," and "envious court" with a more clipped and frosty voice.

Exploit the sonority and alliteration that the next set of lines provide as Duke Senior describes the cold and wind. The phrases in the next section also provide opportunities for physical gestures. Perhaps Duke Senior could pantomime a set of fangs with his index and middle fingers on "icy fang," wag his finger on "churlish chiding," or strike his own chest to illustrate the "bites and blows upon my body." When Duke Senior says, "even till I shrink with cold," he might hunch his shoulders down and hug his chest. Not every phrase has to be physically illustrated, however. Choose the gestures that speak to you. Try standing in front of a mirror or, even better, video record yourself to see the effect your voice and body will have on the audience.

The following Duke Senior line is in quotation marks to indicate that it is something he will say in the future:

> "*This is no flattery. These are counselors*
> *That feelingly persuade me what I am.*"

For this line, you must change your demeanor and tone to make it more presentational. Since Senior describes himself as smiling, be sure to smile and stand a bit straighter. Try extending your arms out, as if welcoming adversity with open arms, and speak the line like you are sharing a revelation you have just had. This speech by Duke Senior is a personal inspiration, but it might also be a "pep talk" to raise the spirits of his men. If you are alone, deliver the lines to an imaginary audience. If you have others with you on stage, look them in the eye and engage them with your words.

When reciting the centerpiece phrase—"Sweet are the uses of adversity"—continue with the revelatory tone of voice that you started with the previous line. You have made a personal discovery with an important lesson you are sharing. You are saying the words for yourself and for an audience of followers. In addition to being a treatise on the power of spirit over hardship, this speech is treatise to the beauty and healing power of nature. When describing the jewel in the venomous toad's head, see if there is a hand gesture that could illustrate this image. One possibility is a simple pinching of the fingers to suggest holding a small gem.

In the final two lines of the monologue, Duke Senior assigns human qualities to natural phenomena. To give a sense of place, gesture toward the trees, brooks, and stones when describing them. Perhaps Duke even picks up a stone and playfully puts it to his ear as if listening to the ocean's roar in a seashell. Clearly, nature speaks to the Duke and provides him with comfort and wisdom. Try to bring the Duke's feelings to the text so that the audience feels them, too. Just as Duke Senior finds "the good in everything," you can find the good in Shakespeare's words as you convey the Duke's love of nature and sunny optimism in the face of adversity.

SUGGESTED VIEWING

AS YOU LIKE IT, 1978
Director: Basil Coleman
Starring: Helen Mirren, Brian Stirner

AS YOU LIKE IT, 2006
Director: Kenneth Branagh
Starring: Bryce Dallas Howard, Romola Garai

✳ THE COMEDY OF ERRORS

CHARACTERS IN THE PLAY

*The following is a list of characters that appear
in this scene of* The Comedy of Errors.

ANTIPHOLUS OF SYRACUSE: Twin of Antipholus of Ephesus
DROMIO OF SYRACUSE: Twin of Dromio of Ephesus; bondsman
to Antipholus
ADRIANA: Wife to Antipholus of Ephesus
LUCIANA: Her sister
NARRATOR

SET AND PROP LIST

SET PIECES:
Bench

PROPS:
Hat for Antipholus

✳ *THE COMEDY OF ERRORS:*
ACT II, SCENE II

Outside of Antipholus of Ephesus's house.

Enter NARRATOR *from stage rear, coming downstage center.*

NARRATOR
> Now Dromio of Syracuse, our first Dromio, comes back and has no idea why Antipholus of Syracuse thinks he was just there. They wind up at the house of Adriana, who thinks Antipholus of Syracuse is actually Antipholus of Ephesus, her husband and his twin—who we haven't met yet. Confused? Good! So are they!

Exit NARRATOR *stage left.*

Enter ANTIPHOLUS OF SYRACUSE *from stage rear; he stands in front of bench.*

ANTIPHOLUS OF SYRACUSE
> The gold I gave to Dromio is laid up
> Safe at the Centaur; I could not speak with Dromio since at first
> I sent him from the mart. See, here he comes.

Enter DROMIO OF SYRACUSE *from stage right.*

ANTIPHOLUS OF SYRACUSE
> How now sir! Is your merry humor alter'd?
> Jest with me again. You received no gold?
> Your mistress sent to have me home to dinner?

DROMIO OF SYRACUSE
> I did not see you since you sent me hence,
> with the gold you gave me.

ANTIPHOLUS OF SYRACUSE
> Think'st thou I jest? Hold, take thou that, and that.
> *(beats* DROMIO *with his hat)*

ANTIPHOLUS *chases* DROMIO *around the bench.*

DROMIO OF SYRACUSE
> But, I pray, sir why am I beaten?

ANTIPHOLUS OF SYRACUSE
> For flouting me.

ANTIPHOLUS *chases* DROMIO *again, hitting him with his hat. The chase ends with both sitting on the bench.*

DROMIO OF SYRACUSE
> Well, sir, I thank you.

ANTIPHOLUS OF SYRACUSE
> Thank me, sir, for what?

DROMIO OF SYRACUSE
> Marry, sir, for this something that you gave me for
> nothing.

Enter ADRIANA *and* LUCIANA *from stage right. As* ADRIANA *approaches* ANTIPHOLUS, DROMIO *gets up and stands behind bench.*

ADRIANA

Ay, ay, Antipholus, look strange and frown.
Some other mistress hath thy sweet aspects.
I am not Adriana, nor thy wife.
The time was once when thou unurged wouldst vow
That never words were music to thine ear,
That never object pleasing in thine eye,
That never touch well welcome to thy hand,
That never meat sweet-savored in thy taste,
Unless I spake, or looked, or touched, or carved to thee.
How comes it now, my husband, O, how comes it
That thou art then estrangèd from thyself?
"Thyself" I call it, being strange to me,
That, undividable, incorporate,
Am better than thy dear self's better part.
Ah, do not tear away thyself from me!
For know, my love, as easy mayst thou fall
A drop of water in the breaking gulf,
And take unmingled thence that drop again
Without addition or diminishing,
As take from me thyself and not me too.
How dearly would it touch thee to the quick,
Shouldst thou but hear I were licentious
And that this body, consecrate to thee,
By ruffian lust should be contaminate!
Wouldst thou not spit at me, and spurn at me,
And hurl the name of husband in my face,
And tear the stained skin off my harlot brow,
And from my false hand cut the wedding ring,
And break it with a deep-divorcing vow?
I know thou canst, and therefore see thou do it.
I am possessed with an adulterate blot;
My blood is mingled with the crime of lust;
For if we two be one, and thou play false,
I do digest the poison of thy flesh,
Being strumpeted by thy contagion.

Keep then fair league and truce with thy true bed,
I live distained, thou undishonorèd.

ANTIPHOLUS OF SYRACUSE *(stands)*
Plead you to me, fair dame? I know you not.

LUCIANA
Fie, brother! How the world is changed with you!
When were you wont to use my sister thus?
She sent for you by Dromio home to dinner.

ANTIPHOLUS OF SYRACUSE
By Dromio?

DROMIO OF SYRACUSE
By me?

ADRIANA
By thee.

ANTIPHOLUS OF SYRACUSE *(to* DROMIO*)*
How can she thus then call us by our names,
Unless it be by inspiration?

ADRIANA *(stands, faces* ANTIPHOLUS*)*
How ill agrees it with your gravity
To counterfeit thus grossly with your slave,
Abetting him to thwart me in my mood!
(tries a gentler approach, holding his arm) Come, I
          will fasten on this sleeve of thine:
Thou art an elm, my husband, I a vine.

LUCIANA
Why pratest thou to thyself and answer'st not?
Dromio, thou drone, thou snail, thou slug, thou sot!

DROMIO OF SYRACUSE (*to* ANTIPHOLUS)
>I am transformed, master; I am an ape.

LUCIANA
>If thou art changed to aught, 'tis to an ass.

DROMIO OF SYRACUSE
>'Tis true; she rides me and I long for grass.
>'Tis so, I am an ass; else it could never be
>But I should know her as well as she knows me.

ANTIPHOLUS OF SYRACUSE
>Am I in earth, in heaven, or in hell?
>Sleeping or waking? Mad or well-advised?
>Known unto these, and to myself disguised!
>I'll say as they say and persever so,
>And in this mist at all adventures go.

DROMIO OF SYRACUSE
>Master, shall I be porter at the gate?

ADRIANA *takes* DROMIO *by the ear and leads him stage right.*

ANTIPHOLUS OF SYRACUSE (*walks downstage center, addressing audience*)
>To me she speaks; she moves me for her theme:
>What, was I married to her in my dream?

ADRIANA
>Ay; and let none enter, lest I break your pate.

DROMIO OF SYRACUSE (*walks downstage center, addressing audience*)
>This is the fairy land: O spite of spites!
>We talk with goblins, owls, and sprites.

LUCIANA

Come, come, Antipholus, we dine too late.

Exit ADRIANA, LUCIANA, *and* ANTIPHOLUS *stage rear.*

DROMIO *looks to stage right entrance, looks to audience, shrugs, and exits stage right.*

✳ *THE COMEDY OF ERRORS:* PERFORMANCE NOTES

I directed this performance of *The Comedy of Errors* in 2004. Like many of the plays I have directed for the Folger Library Student Shakespeare Festival, this production has simple staging. We create a sense of place and character using our bodies and our words, plus a few well-placed musical cues.

Playing courtly music at the top of the first scene sets the mood, and helps define where we are (i.e., at the Duke's palace). Duke Solinus sits on the throne. Egeon is hooded and bound with his hands behind his back, kneeling. Thus with a few props, costumes, and staging ideas we create a strong visual image that contributes to painting the scene, the relationship, and the status of the characters. The actress playing Duke of Solinus wanted to play her character as a female, so we changed the character from "Duke" to "Duchess," which added an interesting dynamic to the play and inspired me to experiment with gender switching in subsequent performances.

In this confusing comedy of mistaken identity featuring two sets of identical twins, if the audience is not clear on the story from the outset, they will remain confused, which will detract from their enjoyment of the play. If the audience understands the story, they can then relax and enjoy the language and the characterizations.

In a comedy, it helps to have moments where the story could take a turn in the other direction, toward violence or tragedy. In general, playing the characters' emotions and conflicts earnestly rather than playing them for laughs will reap the biggest comedic rewards. This way the humor comes from the characters, the language, the action, and the circumstances as they unfold to the audience. We trust that by believing in these elements, the humor will emerge!

There are numerous acting techniques and staging devices that enhance the production, but we must not forget to return to the beauty and power of William Shakespeare's words. Rather than rushing through the speeches, actors must color individual words, and really let them hang in the air, only to fall evocatively on listeners' ears.

The ninth-grade young woman who played Antipholus of Syracuse in our production of *The Comedy of Errors* had a nice clear voice accompanied by crisp gestures. In Act I, Scene II of the play, Antipholus of Syracuse and Dromio of Ephesus share a scene, the first of many mistaken identity scenes, which sets the tone for subsequent hilarious errors. In this scene, the actress playing Antipholus of Syracuse takes great pleasure in beating Dromio of Ephesus with her character's hat. Fortunately, the performer portraying Dromio also took joy in cowering on his back, covering his head with his hands to avoid the beating. For the scene to succeed, the person being beaten must be the one in control. This is broad physical comedy, and it benefits from expansive exaggerated movements from the actors. The farther they take the physical comedy, through commitment to big movements and silliness, the more fun they have with it, and the audience picks up on the merriment.

How do we take it farther? One simple exercise is to play a theatrical moment four different ways: small, normal, bigger, and over the top. "Small" entails purposefully saying one's line in an almost inaudible whisper with little body movement. Most participants agree that there is not much sense in delivering a line that the audience can't hear. "Normal" means "as if one were sitting in a room talking." The actor makes no additional effort to project or enunciate, nor does she try to emote. When an actor recites a line of Shakespeare in "normal" mode, other players usually find this lacking too. Sometimes I point out to them that this is actually what I am seeing and hearing when they think they are performing at the next level: "bigger."

"Bigger" implies a level of exaggeration or stylization that is a hallmark of stage acting: chewing the words, holding a gesture or pose slightly larger and longer than usual, and projecting as if one were trying to reach the back row. It also calls for a greater vocal range: The words take on a more sing-song quality, the pitch gets higher and lower, and the facial expressions are more pronounced. If you are lucky, you will achieve this third level in performance. The final level is the most useful in comedy, but also helpful with beginning actors in any genre: "over the top." In "over the top," I encourage my thespians to throw caution to the wind and see just how big, loud, exaggerated, and ridiculous they can be, without regard to whether it makes sense for the scene. I am essentially asking them to go beyond their perceived limits of decorum. I assure them that it is impossible for them to overact or overemphasize in this exercise. I am asking for systematic and purposeful breaking of boundaries. This is where it gets interesting, because frequently what actors give me at this stage is exactly what I want! Nobody ever goes too far, and what many beginning actors consider "over the top" is actually what I see as the proper level of exaggeration for a silly comedy. The most important lesson to be derived from this exercise is that there is a great range of possibilities and we often don't know what the scope is until we experiment with stretching our limits. This exercise can be applied to just vocals, as well as speech combined with movement.

THE COMEDY OF ERRORS: ACT II, SCENE II

The narrator begins Act II, Scene II by explaining the increasingly convoluted circumstances surrounding the two sets of twins, finally exclaiming, "Confused? Good. So are they!" During rehearsal, we added, "So am I!" as a coda, which got a laugh, partly because it gave the narrator an identity and a personality. Even small roles, in this case a role with no character name, can have charisma and add to the dramatic life of the play.

In this scene, we repeat the comic bit of Antipholus repeatedly striking Dromio with his hat, only this time, it's the other Dromio. They up the ante by chasing each other around the bench; Dromio also slides under the bench to try to avoid being beaten, thus taking the physical comedy one step farther.

Dromio ends up with the hat, and proceeds to hit Antipholus with it. By having Antipholus beat Dromio with his hat for a second time, we establish a physical vocabulary for the comedy. Repetition enhances humor. Having Dromio turn the tables by beating Antipholus with the hat adds a twist to the comedy: the element of surprise. I missed an opportunity here to repeat this comic bit a third time, with yet another twist. Doing so would have gotten a bigger laugh than before, due to comedy's rule of three. Perhaps at the very end of the play as the two sets of twins recited the line, "We came into the world like brother and brother," they could have given each other one more whack on the head with the hat, to put a cap on the comedy!

As Adriana and Luciana enter, Dromio and Antipholus are no longer fighting; they are on the same team. Dromio nudges Antipholus to talk to this woman who believes she is his wife. In this scene, Luciana demonstrates her no-nonsense character with physical poses: crossed arms and defiant posture. On each name she calls Dromio, she pokes him in the chest: "Thou drone," (poke) "thou snail," (poke) "thou slug," (poke) "thou sot," (poke, poke, poke), ultimately backing poor Dromio up against the wall. These physical moves work wonders in accentuating Shakespeare's words and increasing the audience laughter.

When Antipholus exclaims "And in this mist at all adventures go," he raises his sword high and jogs out enthusiastically, following the ladies. Simple, effective blocking and physical gestures, combined with actor enthusiasm, helps players and audience alike gain a better understanding of Shakespeare's text, characters, and relationships. The result is a merry play!

✳ *THE COMEDY OF ERRORS:* MONOLOGUE NOTES

ACT II, SCENE II: ADRIANA MONOLOGUE

In this speech, Adriana beckons the man she thinks is her husband (Antipholus of Ephesus), who is in fact her husband's twin (Antipholus of Syracuse). When he does not recognize her, she launches into a formidable tirade, which aptly paints a portrait of a passionate married woman with strong opinions on the institution of marriage—and a fiery personality to match.

Adriana begins the monologue with sarcasm. When she says, "Look strange and frown," she is not describing what she wishes Antipholus to do. Rather, she is stating her distaste for Antipholus' facial expression, prefacing her remarks with "Ay, ay." She might even imitate his face by facially mirroring Antipholus's blank, confused expression. If playing the speech as part of the scene, you can mimic the face Antipholus is making; if playing the monologue solo, you can simply invent a ridiculous face and express it straight out to the audience. Either way, it will likely get a laugh.

In the second sentence, Adriana's suspicion is immediately evident: "Some other mistress hath thy sweet aspects." The Folger Shakespeare Library notes for *The Comedy of Errors* indicate that the second syllable of "aspects" is emphasized. This will give you the opportunity to really spit out the word, with the sharp "-ects" sound cutting through the air like a knife. Utter it with heartache and fury.

The third sentence continues with derision: "I am not Adriana, nor thy wife."

The words "Adriana" and "thy wife" can be emphasized. Color these words to express Adriana's true feelings. Try saying "thy wife" with anger, and then try the phrase again with pain in your voice. Perhaps both emotions will make their way into the phrase. Study the whole speech and some of Adriana's other earlier speeches in this scene and in Act II, Scene I. Invariably, when you are familiar with a character's arc throughout the whole play, you are better able to deliver a nuanced speech containing that character's many facets. Sadness and anger are evident in Adriana's words. Can you identify any other emotions, perhaps in the subtext? Is there tenderness and love for Antipholus below the sorrow and hurt of perceived infidelity and abandonment?

A shift in tone and content follows the first three lines. Adriana now describes what she and Antipholus had together. She appeals to Antipholus's senses: hearing, sight, touch, and taste, asserting that it was through his love for her that all his senses were enriched. There is an opportunity here for physical gestures. Something as simple as a soft palm-on-palm motion while speaking the word "hand" can convey the more gentle, wistful tone of this passage. Experiment in front of a mirror, and pick one gesture for the passage that you believe will aptly accompany this sensual set of descriptions.

Until the line that begins with "Unless I spake," the speech is exclusively written in iambic pentameter. In this line, however, there is an extra beat: "Un**less** I **spake** or **looked** or **touched,** or **carved**" is one line of iambic pentameter. Thus, the moment before the words "To thee" emerges as a natural "beat" or breathing point. This beat can give weight to the two words and allow Adriana to pour an extra measure of tenderness into them. The iambic pentameter rhythm is like a heartbeat. When the rhythm is off by an extra beat, you can play it as if Adriana's heart has skipped a beat, in this case at the mention of her love, Antipholus.

Next Adriana asks Antipholus a question, which shifts the tone from wistful and gentle to perplexed. Throughout this speech, it is important to note that Adriana is responding to an Antipholus who does not even recognize her. In order for the speech to have its full power, Adriana must react to Antipholus's apparent amnesia at ever having known the woman who he married. Remember to exploit these baffling circumstances to maximize the dramatic impact of this monologue.

Shakespeare uses repetition throughout this passage, which you can use to drive Adriana's point home and give the speech dynamics. The first two words in the monologue are the same: "Ay" and "Ay." Make the second "Ay" louder and more powerful than the first. "That never" is repeated four times in a row. Use that repetition like a hammer, emphasizing Adriana's plight. She repeats "how comes it" twice. When Adriana says something for the second time, you should echo the tone of the first instance but with the intensity raised. She repeats the word "thyself" four times and says "thy dear self" once. In this case, perhaps each instance of the word "thyself" has a slightly different tone, depending on the context in which it is spoken.

The word "self" will sound different when Adriana refers to "thy dear self's better part" than it does when she implores Antipholus not to "tear away thyself from me." Not all repetitions are the same. Study the repeated words and phrases and decide how you will use them to poetic and dramatic ends.

Adriana's exclamation of "Ah, do not tear away thyself from me!" implies that she has either taken Antipholus by the arm or embraced him. If you are playing the scene with another actor, you can physically enact this, but if you are performing the monologue solo, perhaps you could interpret the phrase "tear away" to mean that Antipholus is walking away. If this is the case, you could take a step or two toward him.

This brings up an important point. When speaking to another character in a solo monologue, you must decide where that person is on stage. The character could be the audience as a whole, which can be achieved by looking straight out over the viewers. Another approach is to speak to an imagined person on the stage, presumably to your right or left (or moving across the stage). In the case of Antipholus's "tearing" himself away from Adriana, whether Antipholus is on the stage or placed in the audience, the line indicates movement, so your eyes should follow Antipholus as he moves farther away. You might step closer to him for the next line.

This next line contains the phrase "my love." Here Adriana is expressing how she feels inseparable from Antipholus. This echoes a speech by Antipholus of Syracuse in Act I, Scene II: "I to the world am like a drop of water/That in the ocean seeks another drop."

In his earlier "drop of water" speech, Antipholus of Syracuse refers to his search for his long-lost brother. If playing this scene as a duo, Antipholus could react with recognition to this metaphor as Adriana speaks it, since he himself said similar words regarding his connection with his brother. If Adriana is playing the monologue solo, let the beauty and meaning of the words guide you. Luxuriate in their sound. Don't rush the words. Enjoy them!

The sentence that begins "For know, my love," is a long one—five lines—so you must find beats and breathing points. Find at least two places in the sentence to breathe and gather your vocal strength and tone. Certainly, the words "my love," bracketed in commas, can be one breathing point. Again, use the repeated words ("drop," "take," "me") and use them to give rhythmic and sonic shape to the speech. Perhaps simply emphasizing the repeated words will enhance their poetry.

Next, Adriana turns the tides, reminding Antipholus how he would feel if he suffered Adriana's treatment. The language becomes sharper and harsher. The softness of the previous lines can now contrast with the coarseness of words such as "touch," "quick," "licentious," "ruffian lust," and "contaminate." Emphasize the "s" and "t" sounds as you say them. Give physical illustration to words such as "spit," "spurn," "hurl," "tear," and "cut". Lean your head forward when you say them. Use your arms to depict cutting, hurling, and tearing. This passage gives you an opportunity to show what Adriana feels in her body when she says these strong words.

In the final section of the soliloquy, Adriana again makes herself the subject of her words. This time, however, she does so in relation to Antipholus's perceived misdeeds. She likens Antipholus's infidelity to an infectious disease that stains her inside and out. Again, you can emphasize the sounds of key words such as "blood," "crime," "digest," "poison," "strumpeted," and "contagion."

Adriana's text is full of beautifully descriptive language. If you color key words and phrases to give them their full expression, and study the speech for its poetry, meaning, and feeling, then you will indeed give life to Shakespeare's wonderful depiction of a woman scorned.

SUGGESTED VIEWING

THE COMEDY OF ERRORS, 1978
Director: Phillip Casson
Starring: Judi Dench, Roger Rees

THE COMEDY OF ERRORS, 1983
Director: James Cellan Jones
Starring: Roger Daltrey, Suzanne Bertish

✳ HAMLET

CHARACTERS IN THE PLAY

The following is a list of characters that appear in this scene of Hamlet.

HAMLET: Son of the late King Hamlet
OPHELIA: Daughter to Polonius; sister to Laertes
NARRATOR

SET AND PROP LIST

SET PIECES:
Throne
Chair
Table

PROPS:
Box (or bundle) of letters for Ophelia

✳ *HAMLET:* ACT III, SCENE I

A room in the castle.

Enter NARRATOR *from stage rear, coming downstage center.*

NARRATOR
>Hamlet and Ophelia, the daughter of King
>Claudius's chief officer Polonius, have recently
>confessed their affection for each other. But when
>Ophelia's father, bound by the king to spy on
>Hamlet, orders Ophelia to return Hamlet's love
>letters, the prince's vicious and unhinged reaction
>upsets her greatly.

Exit NARRATOR *stage right.*

Enter HAMLET *from stage right.*

Enter OPHELIA *from stage left, holding letters.*

OPHELIA
>My lord, I have remembrances of yours,
>That I have longed long to re-deliver;
>I pray you, now receive them.

HAMLET
>No, not I;
>I never gave you aught.

OPHELIA
> My honor'd lord, you know right well you did;
> And, with them, words of so sweet breath composed
> As made the things more rich: Their perfume lost,
> Take these again; for to the noble mind
> Rich gifts wax poor when givers prove unkind.
> There, my lord. *(gives letters to* HAMLET*)*

HAMLET *steps in close to* OPHELIA *and turns toward her.*

HAMLET
> I did love you once.

OPHELIA *(takes a step toward* HAMLET*)*
> Indeed, my lord, you made me believe so.

HAMLET *(turns away suddenly)*
> You should not have believed me; I loved you not.

HAMLET *returns the letters to* OPHELIA.

OPHELIA *(hurt)*
> I was the more deceived.

HAMLET *(points at* OPHELIA; *yells)*
> Get thee to a nunnery: Why wouldst thou be a
> breeder of sinners? Or, if thou wilt needs marry,
> marry a fool; for wise men know well enough what
> monsters you make of them. *(points again)* To a
> nunnery, go, and quickly too. Farewell.

HAMLET *begins to exit stage right.*

OPHELIA
> O heavenly powers, restore him!

HAMLET *turns around and comes back toward* OPHELIA.

HAMLET

God has given you one face, and you make
yourselves another. Go to, I'll no more on't; it
hath made me mad. I say, we will have no more
marriages. To a nunnery, go.

Exit HAMLET *stage right.*

OPHELIA

O, what a noble mind is here o'erthrown!
The courtier's, soldier's, scholar's, eye, tongue, sword,
Th' expectancy and rose of the fair state,
The glass of fashion and the mold of form,
Th' observed of all observers, quite, quite down!
And I, of ladies most deject and wretched,
That sucked the honey of his musicked vows,
Now see that noble and most sovereign reason,
Like sweet bells jangled, out of time and harsh;
That unmatched form and stature of blown youth
Blasted with ecstasy. O, woe is me
T' have seen what I have seen, see what I see!

Exit OPHELIA *stage left.*

✳ *HAMLET:* PERFORMANCE NOTES

I directed this performance of *Hamlet* in 2010 with a group of high school seniors. The actress playing Hamlet in our production had wonderful presence, diction, commitment, and emotional delivery, but she tended to "saw the air too much" with her hands (an acting tic that Hamlet decries in his advice to the players). I appreciated her instincts toward physicalization, especially since most beginning actors move too little, but we had to choose specific moments where her arm movements enhanced the text rather than distracted from it. As with many scenes, by simply breaking the speech down moment by moment, we were able to "suit the action to the word, the word to the action."

Living tableaux can provide visual reinforcement for key plot elements and allow the audience to see what happened in an omitted scene. This technique is often very helpful at the beginning of the play, and can be employed during the narrator's introduction to acquaint the audience with key characters and plot elements. Audiences are not nearly as familiar with the story as the actors are. One should not assume the crowd knows the plot. Tell the tale, but also show the story in living color!

Many of the speeches in this play are full of rich imagery, such as the Ghost's in Act I, Scene V. I asked the actress playing the Ghost to focus on the words themselves, how they sounded, and what they evoked. When an actor breaks a speech down to its individual words, she can "color" each expression and paint a beautifully textured scene for the listener. A player must appreciate the sound and feeling of the words as they leave her mouth: "father's," "spirit," "doom'd," "term," "walk," "night," "day," "confined," "fast," "fires," "foul," "crimes," "nature," "burnt," "purged," and "love." Each of these words alone is expressive, and when spoken as part of a line of Shakespeare, they are poetic.

How does one speak "poetically"? The first rule is not to rush the phrases. Many novice actors hurry their lines, which perplexes the audience. Writing down beats and breathing points in the script helps curb this problem. Performers should mark a slash in their text at appropriate breathing points. They can also underline words or syllables that are accentuated, and then experiment with changing the emphasis to hear how this changes a line's meaning.

Actors can also practice "coloring" their words. Think of the word as not just a word, but also an emotion evoker. See if the word can become a poem in itself, with a richness that echoes its sentiment or enhances the image it arouses. Marking beats and coloring words will encourage actors to slow down their speech.

Many of the decisions actors make can spring directly from the text, and I encourage performers to mine the text for clues to help them in their choices. However, the writing itself does not inform all acting choices. In fact, certain acting choices inform the narrative, i.e., they enable actors and audience to view the story in a different light, based on a performance choice an actor makes. That is why it is so helpful to experiment with different interpretations of a scene before making a final choice on how to perform it.

HAMLET: ACT III, SCENE I

Act III, Scene I is a powerful and emotional scene. It is also tricky to act, because the characters' emotions, especially Hamlet's, change rapidly and unpredictably. Hamlet may be acting insane on purpose, a point that the actor and the group can explore in rehearsal. He is certainly rash and emotional. He also says some very cruel words to Ophelia, whom he once loved, according to Hamlet himself. From a staging perspective, I am interested in having the actors' physical movements reflect their emotions. Hamlet could get physical with Ophelia by holding her shoulders and pushing her, which would certainly give her something to get upset about. On the other hand, his words are more hurtful than any shove. For example, Hamlet and Ophelia approach each other until they are almost touching, and then Hamlet turns away on the line, "I love you not."

As Hamlet is exiting, he turns back to Ophelia and walks toward her for the line, "God has given you one face and you make yourselves another." This back-and-forth staging works on two levels: It reinforces the attraction/repulsion dynamic between Hamlet and Ophelia. Also, if Hamlet is indeed pretending to be mad, it paints a convincing portrait of someone who is behaving erratically. Finally on Hamlet's line, "It hath made me mad," Ophelia turns her back on him, as if it is too painful for her to see him this way.

Beginning actors frequently do not know what to do with their bodies while they are on stage. They either move too much or too little. Just as we can vocally color words through inflection, tone, pauses, and pitch, so can we add body movements that add to a word's meaning. On his line, "marry a fool," Hamlet performs a little stutter-step and a hand pose to signify a fool's jest. When Ophelia describes Hamlet's "noble and most sovereign reason, like sweet bells jangled," she lifts her arm up and rings an imaginary bell. Often a simple physical gesture can help an actor put her stamp on a character and make Shakespeare's words her own.

✳ *HAMLET:* MONOLOGUE NOTES

ACT III, SCENE I: OPHELIA MONOLOGUE

It is important to know your character's entire journey throughout the play, even if you are only performing a scene or monologue. When playing this speech by Ophelia, it is helpful to know Ophelia goes mad several scenes later and subsequently drowns herself. Perhaps you can exhibit hints of Ophelia's future breakdown during her emotional response to Hamlet's presumed madness. Experiment with Ophelia's tone. Try speaking as a fully sane person who is upset over the loss of reason in a loved one. Then try the speech as someone who is so distraught that she herself is losing her grip on reason. Is there anything in the text that can aid you in your choice of how to depict Ophelia's mental and emotional state?

Ophelia is still sane during this speech and is bemoaning Hamlet's apparent mental decline as evidenced by his irrational and cruel behavior toward her in the scene. She is hurt, of course. She and Hamlet have been intimate, and first he tells her he loved her once, then immediately denies it. This monologue contains striking irony in her description of Hamlet's madness since she herself goes mad— with fatal consequences.

The monologue can be broken down into four distinct sections, each with its own mood and tone. First, she describes Hamlet's good qualities and laments their absence in his present condition. Second, she describes her own sad state as a result of Hamlet's mistreatment. Third, she describes Hamlet's mental condition in detail. Finally, she restates her own distress.

If you play each of these sections with the appropriate tone, your speech will travel through Ophelia's feelings about Hamlet and their relationship, giving the monologue lively dynamics and strong emotions.

Let's start with the first word: "O." There is a Shakespeare theatre game that I learned from Folger Education, wherein the speaker says the word "O" in several different ways: surprised, horrified, sad, weary, etc. The sound of the word "O" changes with each reading, and indeed the sound of any word in a monologue changes with the textual and emotional interpretation you choose.

Experiment with two or three different ways of saying "O": shock, dismay/sadness, and, just for variety, anger. How does that change the sound of the word? Think about what has just happened: Hamlet has verbally abused Ophelia. Perhaps, as some renditions have chosen, he even threw her to the ground. If you are playing this monologue as part of the scene, you can react to what has just happened on the stage. If you are playing the monologue alone, you may summon a reaction based upon what you imagine has just happened.

Notice how many times the letter "o" appears in the first two lines: "O", "noble" "o'erthrown," "soldier's," "scholar's," "tongue," and "sword." This gives you an opportunity to find a place to echo or restate the "o" sound, not only for poetic reasons but also for emotional ones. Pick two more "o" sounds to emphasize. Words that immediately come to mind are "noble" and "o'erthrown," but you should experiment to see if any others resonate with you.

With each descriptive word in the second line, Ophelia describes Hamlet's qualities in terms of the roles he plays: courtier, soldier, and scholar. The second part of the sentence attaches a body part or object to each role. Oddly, they are not in the right order. You must look at the speech and attach the corresponding body part or object to its role. The first role, "courtier," matches with the first descriptor, "eye." However, the second role is "soldier," and the second descriptor is "tongue," which actually applies to "scholar."

Should you wish to add a gesture to each word, first try doing so with the roles (courtier, soldier, scholar) and then try the gesture again, this time with the body part or object: (eye, sword, tongue.) The key here is that you have options to work with; by experimenting with alternate gestures and vocal interpretations, you might unearth a fresh view of the text.

For the next three lines, Ophelia extols Hamlet's virtues. Note that she is listing his good qualities directly on the heels of suffering his abuse; this says a lot about her character and her opinion of Hamlet. There could be a bittersweetness to her descriptions, since these are attributes that seem to have now disappeared.

Experiment with saying these three lines (beginning with "Th'expectancy" and ending with "observers") in two ways. First say them as if Ophelia is happily in love with Hamlet and enumerating his good points. Second, utter them sadly, as if mourning the loss of these qualities. Finally, see if you can keep some of the initial joy of the first reading so that your description of Hamlet is at once regretful of loss and remembering happiness. You may end up choosing a delivery that is more definitively mournful, but I still suggest trying alternate interpretations because it is a good way to discover nuances in the character and the monologue.

The words "quite, quite down!" echo the "o" sounds we explored earlier in the speech. Perhaps you could draw the "o" sound on "down" to parallel an emotion-provoking sound you made earlier. Notice how in the next two lines (the second of four sections in this speech wherein Ophelia describes her heartbroken state), the hard consonant "k" and "d" sounds repeat themselves: "de**j**ect," "wretche**d**," "su**ck**ed," and "musi**ck**ed." Shakespeare has a way of painting an emotional picture with the sound of his words. If you utter these sounds with that awareness, your speech will resonate with color and emotional impact.

In the third section, Ophelia describes Hamlet's present mental condition. She begins by referring again to one of Hamlet's positive traits: "that noble and most sovereign reason." Notice how every line in the speech except this one is written in iambic pentameter. "Now see that noble and most sovereign reason" has an extra syllable. Think of the iambic pentameter's rhythm as a heartbeat. When the speaker is in a heightened emotional state, the heart skips a beat. Look at when the iambic pentameter loses its rhythm and see if that provides you with an opportunity for a dramatic beat. This might simply be a pause before the word "reason."

Ophelia describes Hamlet's "madness" and a few scenes later she goes mad herself. This might be an opportunity for you as an actor to show flashes of Ophelia's impending insanity. Hamlet's abuse of her in this scene is the first real trigger of her decline. When describing Hamlet's madness, traces of mental instability might show in Ophelia's face.

How does one portray someone heading toward madness? Let's start with the imagery of the bells. When Ophelia says "Like sweet bells jangled, out of time and harsh" she could lift her hands up to her ears as if hearing something loud. On the words "blasted with ecstasy," Ophelia might widen her eyes, perhaps breaking into a grimace or grin. It might help to look in a mirror or videotape yourself when trying these physical gestures and facial expressions. Over-exaggerate the gestures and expressions to a grotesque level, then bring them back down. Find a level of "expressed madness" that fits the words and the scene.

The final sentence begins with the syllable "O" repeated twice, which can provide a nice symmetry to the monologue. Is it the same "O" that we started the speech with or is it completely different? After the first "O," Ophelia laments Hamlet's condition. By the final "O," she is bemoaning her own condition: "O, woe is me." Although this is not a particularly long monologue, the phrases are rich in poetic imagery and emotion, and it can be a vehicle for you to further the story of one of Shakespeare's great tragic heroines.

SUGGESTED VIEWING

HAMLET, 1948
Director: Laurence Olivier
Starring: Laurence Olivier, Jean Simmons

HAMLET, 1976
Director: Celestino Coronado
Starring: David Meyer, Hellen Mirren

✳ HENRY IV, PART 1

CHARACTERS IN THE PLAY

The following is a list of characters that appear in this scene of Henry IV, Part 1.

KING HENRY IV: Father to Prince Henry; formerly Henry of Bollingbroke

PRINCE HENRY: Also called Harry or Hal; oldest son to King Henry IV

NARRATOR

SET AND PROP LIST

SET PIECES:
Throne

✳ *HENRY IV, PART 1:* ACT III, SCENE II

London. The palace.

Enter **NARRATOR** *from stage right, coming downstage center.*

NARRATOR
>Prince Hal reconciles with his father, King Henry IV,
>by swearing to fight the rebels and to defeat Hotspur.

Exit **NARRATOR** *stage right.*

Enter **KING HENRY IV** *and* **PRINCE HENRY** *from stage left.* **KING HENRY IV** *sits on the throne.*

KING HENRY IV
>I know not whether God will have it so,
>For some displeasing service I have done,
>But thou dost in thy passages of life
>Make me believe that thou art only mark'd
>For the hot vengeance and the rod of heaven
>To punish my mistreadings. Tell me else,
>Could such inordinate and low desires,
>Such barren pleasures, rude society,
>As thou art match'd withal and grafted to,
>Accompany the greatness of thy blood
>And hold their level with thy princely heart?

PRINCE HENRY
>So please your majesty
>Find pardon on my true submission. *(kneels)*

KING HENRY IV

> God pardon thee! Yet let me wonder, Harry,
> At thy affections, which do hold a wing
> Quite from the flight of all thy ancestors.
> The hope and expectation of thy time
> Is ruin'd. Harry, thou has lost thy princely privilege
> With vile participation: Not an eye
> But is a-weary of thy common sight,
> Save mine, which hath desired to see thee more.

PRINCE HENRY *(touched and surprised)*

> I shall hereafter be more myself.

KING HENRY IV

> For all the world
> Percy now leads ancient lords and reverend bishops on
> To bloody battles and to bruising arms.
> Thrice hath this Hotspur, Mars in swathling clothes,
> Discomfited great Douglas, ta'en him once,
> And what say you to this? Percy, Northumberland,
> The Archbishop's grace of York, Douglas, Mortimer,
> Capitulate against us and are up.

PRINCE HENRY

> I will redeem all this on Percy's head,
> And, in the closing of some glorious day,
> Be bold to tell you that I am your son,
> When I will wear a garment all of blood
> And stain my favors in a bloody mask,
> Which, washed away, shall scour my shame with it.
> And that shall be the day, whene'er it lights,
> That this same child of honor and renown,
> This gallant Hotspur, this all-praisèd knight,
> And your unthought-of Harry chance to meet.
> For every honor sitting on his helm,
> Would they were multitudes, and on my head

My shames redoubled! For the time will come
That I shall make this northern youth exchange
His glorious deeds for my indignities.
This in the name of God I promise here,
The which if He be pleased I shall perform,
I do beseech your Majesty may salve
The long-grown wounds of my intemperance.
If not, the end of life cancels all bands,
And I will die a hundred thousand deaths
Ere break the smallest parcel of this vow.

KING HENRY IV *stands and helps* PRINCE HENRY *to his feet. They hold a long handshake and eye contact.*

KING HENRY IV

A hundred thousand rebels die in this:
Thou shalt have charge and sovereign trust herein.

Exit KING HENRY IV *stage right.* PRINCE HENRY *follows.*

✳ *HENRY IV, PART 1:* PERFORMANCE NOTES

I directed this performance of *Henry IV, Part 1* in 2008 with a group of high school seniors. Young actors love this production for its generational conflicts. The clash between the older and younger characters is particularly attractive to adolescents and young adults.

As detailed in the "Performing Shakespeare" essay, performers and directors can use Wordle.net (www.wordle.net/create) to create a "word cloud" graphic that emphasizes which words appear with greatest frequency in a character's speech. Actors can use this information to color their words and shape their characters. What others say about a Shakespearean character provides additional clues as to his nature—and allows us to a portray a three-dimensional living, breathing person, with faults as well as good qualities, i.e., someone like ourselves!

HENRY IV, PART 1: ACT III, SCENE II

Interestingly, art imitated life in this short scene (Act III, Scene II) during our production of *Henry IV, Part 1.* The actor playing Hal in this scene had recently been expelled from school and then reinstated. He had just spent a lot of time apologizing for his behavior, and now he was playing a son apologizing for the same. Needless to say, I encouraged him to use recent occurrences as inspiration as his character begged for his father's pardon.

We do not always have the opportunity for the play's exact mirroring of our own experiences, but with a bit of searching, it is not difficult to find conflicts in our own lives or others' that are similar to those in Shakespeare's texts. Sometimes it takes imagination or a metaphorical leap. In this particular case, the young actor playing Hal simply had to act the same way he had been acting in his real life: genuinely contrite and apologetic. When he stood up and looked straight out at the audience, saying, "This, in the name of God, I promise here," I believed he meant it.

There is no secret answer to how to prevent the unexpected in theater, nor are we guaranteed the audience response we desire. But by delving into the text, committing to the characters, and playing with passion, your group can deliver a production that not only brings joy and satisfaction to audiences, but also builds performers' confidence, opening them up to the vivid worlds that Shakespeare creates. *Henry IV, Part 1* is a magnificent story of a young king and his friends—but it is also a story about how we all grow up and, in doing so, change.

✳ HENRY IV, PART 1: MONOLOGUE NOTES

ACT III, SCENE II: PRINCE HAL MONOLOGUE

The first three words in this monologue—"I will redeem"—set the tone for what is to follow: Prince Hal's promise to turn his shame into glory at Hotspur's expense. It is important to know how Hal has behaved up until this point: wasting his time in the company of drunkards. However, there have been hints that this was not the "real" Prince Hal or at least not his sum total.

When performing a monologue, it is essential to know where the character has been and what has brought him to this point. The monologue might stand alone when you perform it, but to give the piece justice, you must familiarize yourself with the character within the context of the entire play.

In Act I, Scene II, Prince Hal expounds, "I'll so offend to make offense a skill/Redeeming time when men think least I will." Likewise, in Act II, Scene IV, when Falstaff and Hal have been role-playing and Hal play-acts the role of his father, King Henry, Falstaff proclaims, "Banish plump Jack, and banish all the world." Prince Hal then responds prophetically, "I do. I will." Hal's monologue represents the turning point that Shakespeare has hinted at; Prince Hal is going to seize his birthright and his destiny and redeem his past shames.

Hal must convince his father, King Henry, that he can and will change. Remember that this is both a private talk between a father and son and one between a ruler and his heir. To make his case, Hal uses strong words that require emphasis and color. Prince Hal's bad reputation is represented by words like "stain," "scour," and "shame." These stand in contrast to the words he uses to describe his future: "glorious," "bold," "honor," and "renown."

How do Prince Hal's face, body, and voice express these contrasting images? Perhaps he looks down when discussing his shame. When he speaks of what will happen when he meets Percy, known as Hotspur, he might look his father directly in the eye and shows his true confidence and fire. Between Hal's past and future is the day of redemption: "And that shall be the day, whene'er it lights." Hal can imagine that day and picture the sun rising. How does a sunrise look and feel when it is a day you have been waiting for your whole life? Show this in your eyes, and let it ring in your voice.

Hal contrasts Percy's honor with his own shame. In the notes included with the Folger edition of the text, the phrase "every honor sitting on his helm" is explained as "Hal imagines them as insignia worn on Hotspur's helmet and contrasts them with the shames worn on his own." This reminds me of when I first played tackle football in the seventh grade; our coach, who was a cool high school football player, would put gold stars on our helmets for outstanding play. I remember how it felt to get a gold star.

If you can find a personal connection to the images painted by your character's words, you will be able to personalize your monologue and bring your own life experience into it. As mentioned in the performing notes, when we performed the scene with a group of high school students, the young actor playing Hal had just narrowly escaped being expelled from school and had likely had an emotional exchange with his father similar to the one between Prince Hal and King Henry. We have all had parents and thus have personal experiences we can bring to this scene.

Study the text carefully to glean clues on how to play the speech. It is important to note that Hal uses words with typically positive connotations to describe his enemy, Hotspur: "honor," "renown," "gallant," and "all-praised." Hal could spit the words out with contempt or draw them out exaggeratedly. He might choke up on one of the words. King Henry has not only compared his son Hal unfavorably to Hotspur, but he has also insinuated that Hal might actually join Hotspur in a fight against the King "to show how much thou art degenerate." Would this not hurt a son's feelings? Experiment by performing some of Hal's lines with emotions such as contrite, hurt, angry, or bold.

The hurt might turn to anger and willfulness as Hal predicts that he will exchange Hotspur's "glorious deeds" for his "indignities." Thus the monologue can have several phases, moving from contrition through anger, boldness, and finally to the promise of loyalty. Hal's words and phrases in the final lines of the speech portray assurance—"This in the name of God I promise here . . . I do beseech your Majesty"—and end with the strong pledge, "And I will die a hundred thousand deaths/Ere break the smallest parcel of this vow."

These are the words of a Prince Hal quite changed from the carousing Hal of the tavern. They are the oaths of a prince ready to redeem his past transgressions and willing to die for King and country. Portray Hal's dramatic personal transformation in your performance of Shakespeare's moving words.

SUGGESTED VIEWING

THE HOLLOW CROWN
Season 1, Episode 2, 2012
Director: Richard Eyre
Starring: Jeremy Irons, Tom Hiddleston

HENRY IV, PART 1
Royal Shakespeare Company, 2014
Director: Gregory Doran
Starring: Jasper Britton, Alex Hassell

✳ JULIUS CAESAR

CHARACTERS IN THE PLAY

The following is a list of characters that appear in this scene of Julius Caesar.

CHORUS
BRUTUS: A high-ranking nobleman
PORTIA: Brutus's wife
CASSIUS
CASCA
CINNA
DECIUS BRUTUS   Patricians; conspirators against Caesar
METELLUS CIMBER
TREBONIUS

SET AND PROP LIST

SET PIECES:
Chair

PROPS:
Swords

✳ *JULIUS CAESAR:* ACT II, SCENE I

Rome. BRUTUS'S *orchard.*

Enter NARRATOR *from stage rear, coming downstage center.*

NARRATOR
>Brutus and the other conspirators decide to kill
>Caesar but spare Antony. Portia begs Brutus, her
>husband, to explain his change in mood. Storm
>clouds gather.

Exit NARRATOR *stage left.*

STAGE LEFT CHORUS *make sounds of thunder;* STAGE RIGHT
CHORUS *make sounds of rain.*

Enter BRUTUS *from stage right.*

BRUTUS
>It must be by his death: And for my part,
>I know no personal cause to spurn at him,
>But for the general. He would be crown'd:
>It is the bright day that brings forth the adder;

STAGE RIGHT CHORUS *gesture upward;* STAGE LEFT CHORUS
gesture downward.

>Therefore think him as a serpent's egg
>Which, hatch'd, would, as his kind, grow mischievous,
>And kill him in the shell.

CHORUS *gesture in unison.*

SOUND OPERATOR *plays* Sound Cue #1 ("Knocking").

> They are the faction. O conspiracy,
> Where wilt thou find a cavern dark enough
> To mask thy monstrous visage?

Enter from stage right the CONSPIRATORS: CASSIUS, CASCA, DECIUS BRUTUS, CINNA, METELLUS CIMBER, *and* TREBONIUS.

BRUTUS

> Give me your hands all over, one by one.

CONSPIRATORS *bring hands in, forming a circle.*

CASSIUS

> And let us swear our resolution.

CONSPIRATORS *remove hands from circle.*

DECIUS BRUTUS

> Shall no man else be touch'd but only Caesar?

CASSIUS

> Let Antony and Caesar fall together.

BRUTUS

> Our course will seem too bloody, Caius Cassius,
> To cut the head off and then hack the limbs,
> For Antony is but a limb of Caesar:
> Let's kill him boldly, but not wrathfully;
> Which so appearing to the common eyes,
> We shall be call'd purgers, not murderers.

CASSIUS

> Yet I fear him;
> For in the ingrafted love he bears to Caesar—

SOUND OPERATOR *plays* Sound Cue #2 ("Clock striking three").

> The clock hath stricken three.

TREBONIUS
> 'Tis time to part.

Exit ALL *but* BRUTUS *stage right.*

Exit CHORUS, *splitting down the middle to exit stage right and stage left.*

Enter PORTIA *from stage left.*

PORTIA
> Brutus, my lord!

BRUTUS
> Portia, what mean you? Wherefore rise you now?

PORTIA *(moving close to* BRUTUS*)*
> You've ungently, Brutus, stole from my bed:
> And when I ask'd you what the matter was,
> You stared upon me and stamp'd with your foot;
> Dear my lord,
> Make me acquainted with your cause of grief.

BRUTUS *(moving away from* PORTIA *toward stage right)*
> I am not well in health, and that is all.

PORTIA
> Is Brutus sick? And is it physical
> To walk unbracèd and suck up the humors
> Of the dank morning? What, is Brutus sick,
> And will he steal out of his wholesome bed
> To dare the vile contagion of the night
> And tempt the rheumy and unpurgèd air

To add unto his sickness? No, my Brutus,
You have some sick offense within your mind,
Which by the right and virtue of my place
I ought to know of. And, upon my knees,

PORTIA *kneels.*

I charm you, by my once-commended beauty,
By all your vows of love, and that great vow
Which did incorporate and make us one,
That you unfold to me, your self, your half,
Why you are heavy, and what men tonight
Have had resort to you; for here have been
Some six or seven who did hide their faces
Even from darkness.

(IF PERFORMING MONOLOGUE SOLO, OMIT BRACKETED LINES AND CONTINUE
WITH PORTIA'S SPEECH.)

[BRUTUS
Kneel not, gentle Portia.

He lifts her up.]

PORTIA
[I should not need, if you were gentle Brutus.]
Within the bond of marriage, tell me, Brutus,
Is it excepted I should know no secrets
That appertain to you? Am I your self
But, as it were, in sort or limitation,
To keep with you at meals, comfort your bed,
And talk to you sometimes? Dwell I but in the
        suburbs
Of your good pleasure? If it be no more,
Portia is Brutus' harlot, not his wife.

BRUTUS *(turning* PORTIA *around)*
> You are my true and honorable wife,
> As dear to me as are the ruddy drops
> That visit my sad heart.

PORTIA
> If this were true, then should I know this secret.

BRUTUS *(looking up)*
> O ye gods,
> Render me worthy of this noble wife!
> *(gestures left)* Portia, go in awhile;
> And by and by thy bosom shall partake
> The secrets of my heart.

BRUTUS *begins to exit stage left, crossing in front of* PORTIA. *He turns back toward her.*

> Follow me, then.

Exit BRUTUS *stage left, with* PORTIA *following.*

✳ JULIUS CAESAR: PERFORMANCE NOTES

I directed this performance of *Julius Caesar* in 2012 with a group of high school seniors. Most notable about this particular production was that I used a Chorus for the first time. The Chorus provides a way for actors who would otherwise only have minor parts to become integral to the play and appear in several scenes. This contributed greatly to the overall feel of the performance as an ensemble production. The Chorus provided visual and sound effects, verbal commentary, and emotional reactions to the action on the stage. By doing so, the Chorus makes it easier for audiences to follow the plot and themes of the play, which not only helped clarify the story, but also added to its power. I will most certainly try to find use for the Chorus in subsequent productions. Note that when on stage, the Chorus is divided into two parts: Stage Right and Stage Left Chorus. The two sides form a "V" shape, which allows for better visibility and mirroring of each other's movements.

The Chorus provides sound effects beginning early on in the play. Live music, even in the absence of real musical instruments, imparts a feeling that pre-recorded sounds cannot. Not only does it engage the actors, but it has an immediacy and power all its own. Whenever possible, enlist the actors to provide live sound effects.

There are several moments in this play where the Chorus provides tableaux, either a mobile tableau to accompany smaller phrases or a fixed tableau to illustrate a larger passage. The tableau is an effective snapshot for helping audiences understand the scene, and it nudges actors to look deeper into the text, knowing that they have to provide a stage picture to represent it. Your cast can develop a physical vocabulary for this by participating in theater games in early rehearsals; choose small groups of four or five actors to present tableaux that illustrate portions of text.

Given that this play revolves around Caesar's murder, fight scenes were an essential element. Scenes containing stage combat, killings, or any sort of swordplay require a respect for the dangers inherent therein. Actors should be taught not to play with the weapons or use them outside of specific rehearsals, even if the swords are wooden or plastic. Because young actors tend to fidget with swords and daggers and wave them about randomly, I avoid using them as simple costume pieces and save them for their intended uses: fighting and killing. I have been fortunate to enlist my colleague, professional actor Michael Tolaydo, to stage fights in several of my productions, but a professional is not always available. A very effective technique for safely staging fight and murder scenes is slow motion.

If a tragedy does not have any moments of outright comic relief, I try to provide one or two in the narration or staging. Narrator lines are an apt place for comic relief because, since we are between episodes, one does not risk undercutting the emotion of the scene. Shakespeare, of course, inserted bits of comic relief into many of his tragedies, but if the cutting or the play itself lacks laugh lines, then we can create them ourselves. Audiences need a moment of release before they dive back into the deep end of a Shakespearean tragedy.

JULIUS CAESAR: ACT II, SCENE I

At the narrator's final line of this scene (Act II, Scene I), "Storm clouds gather," members of the Chorus waved their hands in front of them to indicate wind, while the sound operator made recorder whistle and drum sounds. As the recorder and drum sounds play, the Chorus and sound operator's sonic and physical repetitions provide a nonverbal tonal palette against which the words and actions unfold.

This scene offers opportunities for the Chorus to illustrate the text; they do so here by creating moving tableaux that illustrate specific phrases. On "think of him as a serpent's egg, which hatch'd would . . . kill him in the shell," I asked the Chorus members to suggest some moves for this line, and one actor did such an artful job of physically depicting the text that I assigned her the role of Chorus Captain.

Our Chorus Captain snaked her arm up on "a serpents' egg, which hatch'd" and then brought it down swiftly to her midsection as if to stab herself on "would . . . kill him in the shell," simultaneously bending at the waist and lowering her head as if dying. To enhance this effect, the sound operator played a small shaker to suggest the hissing of a snake. It is amazing how much small details like this can add to a scene's mood and visual palette. (It is wise, however, not to overdo the sound cues. As with scene changes and set pieces, they should be used sparingly; if the production becomes overly complex, the stage crew and actors will be distracted from the more pressing business of tale telling.)

Recalling an incident from a staging of *Macbeth* several years prior, when an actor simply refused to go on with the scene until she heard a "shrieking owl," I had impressed upon the *Julius Caesar* cast the importance of continuing on in the absence of a sound cue. In this case, the sound operator was to hit a musical triangle three times to indicate chiming prior to the line "the clock hath stricken three." When he neglected to hit the triangle at the proper point, there was only a brief pause, and the actor portraying Cassius wisely proceeded with her line. Always remember that in the face of miscues, absent sound effects, or any other stage mishaps: Keep going. In fact, I would have preferred that the conspirators cock their heads as if listening to the chiming of a clock, but I was satisfied that they continued and did not let a flubbed sound cue derail the scene.

The second half of this scene features dialogue between Brutus and Portia that nicely illustrates their relationship. It is a dance of approach and avoidance, based on the predominant sentiment of each phrase being spoken. Portia moves toward Brutus on "Make me acquainted with your cause of grief," and Brutus moves away from Portia on "I am not well in health and that is all." Explore the couple's relationship by examining the text and finding words, phrases, and moments that can be enhanced by a movement, gesture, facial expression, or vocal inflection.

While the actor playing Portia wanted to turn her back fully on Brutus (and the audience) on the line "If it be no more, Portia is Brutus's harlot, not his wife," I encouraged her to speak and then turn, since to do so simultaneously would muffle her words. She forgot this note during performance, turning her back to the audience while saying the line, which greatly lessened its effect. This kind of staging error can easily be remedied for subsequent performances. In our case, we only had one performance of the play and were unable to fix it for later. That's showbiz.

Explore the richness and variety inherent in every acting and staging choice. Always come back to the text itself for clues. Portia uses the words "ungently," "sick," "once-commended," "heavy," and "harlot." Each of these words has an emotional connotation that can be enhanced physically or verbally. Once actors have explored both the meaning and feeling of the words, they can make choices that make the characters their own.

The group worked as a team, and their dedication and commitment resulted in a *Julius Caesar* that was at once personal and universal. The cast tells a powerful tale, and as their reward, they own a piece of history.

✳ *JULIUS CAESAR:* MONOLOGUE NOTES

ACT II, SCENE I: PORTIA MONOLOGUE

Brutus has informed Portia that he is "not well in health," which is why he left their bed and started walking outside on a stormy night. (The audience, of course, knows that he has gone to meet with the Conspirators.) Portia suspects something, so she begins this speech with the following words: "Is Brutus sick?" It would seem that this question is sarcastic, since she follows it with two rhetorical questions regarding the health benefits of nighttime strolling in bad weather. She then proceeds to answer her own question before Brutus can. The structure and tone of these words paint a picture of Portia as a woman who has strong opinions and is unafraid to voice them openly with her husband.

Playing Portia, you have a choice of tone here. The questions are presumably rhetorical (since she answers them herself) and seemingly sardonic. Portia can skew the tone in a number of possible directions: playful, angry, concerned, sympathetic, or disappointed. There are often clues within the text that help an actor decide which dominant tone to adopt. If the monologue itself does not yield enough information, look deeper into the text. Examine other scenes that feature Portia, or look at what Brutus says about Portia to determine the nature of their relationship. Remember that monologues do not stand alone; they always exist within the context of the whole play.

After Portia's final line of this speech, in which she suggests that "Portia is Brutus' harlot, not his wife," Brutus replies: "You are my true and honorable wife/As dear to me as the ruddy drops/That visit my sad heart."

Later in the scene, Portia says to Brutus:

> *Think you I am no stronger than my sex?*
> *Tell me your counsels: I will not disclose 'em.*
> *I have made strong proof of my constancy,*
> *Giving myself a voluntary wound*
> *Here, in the thigh. Can I bear that with patience,*
> *And not my husband's secrets?*

Brutus replies:

> *O you gods,*
> *Render me worthy of this noble wife!*

By examining beyond the monologue itself, we now discover more qualities about Brutus, Portia, and their relationship. These help determine how to play the scene.

The previous interchanges indicate that 1) Portia is "true," "honorable," and "dear" to Brutus; 2) Brutus's heart is "sad"; 3) Portia considers herself "stronger than my sex," "constant," "patient," and trustworthy; and 4) Brutus describes Portia as "noble."

Having now mined the text for clues as to Brutus and Portia's relationship, we return to the original monologue with a fuller picture of who they are as characters. We are ready to make better-informed decisions as to how to play the speech. The original question was, "What tone do we adopt for Portia's initial rhetorical questions?" Given the solidity of their relationship and their open communication, I suggest playing those "sarcastic" questions with a softness and compassion behind them rather than overt hostility and antagonism, which could be the case if Shakespeare's words had depicted a more toxic spousal relationship.

Portia uses colorful words to describe the unhealthy night air: "dank," "vile," "contagion," "rheumy," "unpurged," and "sickness." Decide which, if any, of these dramatic words to emphasize; you might even choose to accentuate other words in the sentence. Perhaps the word "add" is emphasized, since Portia is making a case for why it would not make sense for Brutus to be out on this cold and stormy night if it would **add** to his malaise. Speak the sentences out loud, stressing different words to see what makes the most sense and has the most theatrical impact. It is through verbal experimentation that the best oratorical decisions emerge!

Portia now answers her own questions: "No, my Brutus/You have some sick offense within your mind." This is Portia's fourth use of the word "sick." She also uses the word "suck" once. Whenever a word or sound is used multiple times, this helps shape the monologue by anchoring it to a repeating tone. Take advantage of alliteration and other poetic words by emphasizing their sound. Bounce off the letter "k" with your tongue as if you were a drummer. Since the sickness Portia now refers to is mental, it makes sense to also emphasize "within your mind."

On the line that begins with "And, upon my knees, I charm you," Portia kneels. Is it a subservient kneeling or more of an imploring kneel? Based on our study of Portia's relationship with Brutus, the latter seems more likely. Portia is concerned about Brutus's activities and his mental state, and she is insisting that he share his situation with her. The tone shifts to a more serious and earnest plea from Portia for Brutus to "unfold" to her why he is "heavy." Here is where we perceive the deep bond Portia feels for Brutus in marriage, invoking the vows that made them one.

Again you should exploit the repetition of the word "vow" for dramatic and poetic effect. Emphasize the phrase "vows of love" and "that great vow" as you look into Brutus's eyes. Stress the words "what" and "why." Portia wants answers because she cares deeply about Brutus and she sees that something is amiss.

When Portia says the phrase, "what men have had resort to you," the tone becomes even more dire. She is telling Brutus that she knows something has transpired between Brutus and these men and that he hides dark secrets.

If you are playing this monologue in the context of the scene, continue with Brutus's line, "Kneel not gentle Portia" as well as Portia's line, "I should not need, if you were gentle Brutus." If you are playing the speech solo, skip those lines and continue with "Within the bond of marriage . . ."

The monologue closes as it opens, with a series of rhetorical questions. Perhaps these questions are not as gentle as those at the beginning of the speech. Brutus has not yet shared any information with Portia, so the stakes are higher. Her patience might be thinning. Perhaps the sarcasm in her tone is harsher. Portia could stand and move away from Brutus to highlight this change in mood. Try these final lines with anger in your voice. Try them again with hurt as the dominant emotion. What effect do these different readings have on your performance? Your interpretation might incorporate anger and hurt while retaining some of the compassionate softness of Portia's original questions.

A monologue works best when it has an arc, a direction from one dynamic to another. If Portia's speech starts with a softness and gentleness and ends with a more urgent and pained feeling, you can increase the dramatic force of her words. Always look to the text for answers. Portia's final two sentences in the speech indicate a greater frustration with her relationship with Brutus. They refer specifically to her own status in the marriage, whereas the original questions concerned only Brutus. The word "harlot" is a strong and harsh word. Spit it out with passion, and contrast it with the strong feelings that Portia evokes when she says the word "wife."

A few moments after the monologue ends, Portia stabs herself in the thigh, and she ultimately kills herself by eating hot coals. Let this vivid and troubling image inform your depiction of Portia in this scene. She may in fact have a "sickness" of her own. Portia is a passionate and strong woman with a deep attachment to her husband Brutus. Bring her noble dignity to life with Shakespeare's words.

SUGGESTED VIEWING

JULIUS CAESAR, 1953
Director: Joseph L. Mankiewicz
Starring: Marlon Brando, John Gielgud, Deborah Kerr

JULIUS CAESAR, 1970
Director: Stuart Burge
Starring: Charlton Heston, John Gielgud, Diana Rigg

* KING LEAR

CHARACTERS IN THE PLAY

The following is a list of characters that appear in this scene of King Lear.

KING LEAR: King of Britain
KENT: Earl of Kent, a loyal subject to King Lear
GLOUCESTER: Earl of Gloucester, father to Edgar
EDGAR: son to the Earl of Gloucester
FOOL
NARRATOR

SET AND PROP LIST

SET PIECES:
Shelter

PROPS:
Torch for Gloucester
Crown for King Lear
Hat for Edgar

✳ *KING LEAR:* ACT III, SCENE IV

The heath, before a hovel.

Enter **NARRATOR** *from stage rear, coming downstage center.*

NARRATOR
> Lear, Kent, and the Fool reach the hovel, where they
> find Edgar disguised as Poor Tom, a madman and
> beggar. When Gloucester finds them, he leads them
> to the shelter of a house. It seems as if Lear is not the
> only one whose sanity is slipping away!

Exit **NARRATOR** *stage right.*

Enter **KING LEAR**, **KENT**, *and the* **FOOL** *from stage left.*

SOUND OPERATOR *plays Sound Cue #1 ("Storm sounds").*

KENT *(holds onto* **LEAR**, *attempting to shelter him from the storm)*
> Here is the place, my lord; good my lord, enter:
> The tyranny of the open night's too rough
> For nature to endure.

KING LEAR *(to* **KENT***)*
> Thou think'st 'tis much that this contentious storm
> Invades us to the skin. So 'tis to thee.
> But where the greater malady is fixed,
> The lesser is scarce felt. Thou'dst shun a bear,
> But if thy flight lay toward the roaring sea,
> Thou'dst meet the bear i' th' mouth. When the
>   mind's free,

The body's delicate. This tempest in my mind
Doth from my senses take all feeling else
Save what beats there. Filial ingratitude!
Is it not as this mouth should tear this hand
for lifing food to 't? But I will punish home.
No, I will weep no more. In such a night
To shut me out? Pour on. I will endure.
In such a night as this? O Regan Goneril,
Your old kind father whose frank heart gave all!
O, that way madness lies. Let me shun that;
No more of that.

KENT

Good my lord, enter here.

KING LEAR

Prithee, go in thyself: seek thine own ease:

The FOOL *walks behind stage left pillar as if entering the hovel.*

This tempest will not give me leave to ponder
On things would hurt me more. But I'll go in.

EDGAR *(within)*

Fathom and half, fathom and half! Poor Tom!

FOOL *(running out from behind pillar)*

Come not in here, nuncle, here's a spirit
Help me, help me!

The FOOL *runs to* KING LEAR'S *side and kneels.* KING LEAR, KENT, *and the* FOOL *huddle together, facing the stage left pillar.*

KENT

Give me thy hand. Who's there?

FOOL

A spirit, a spirit: He says his name's Poor Tom.

KENT

Come forth.

Enter EDGAR, *disguised.*

EDGAR

Away! The foul fiend follows me!

KING LEAR, *fascinated by the madman, slowly approaches*
EDGAR. *The* FOOL, *circling around stage rear, is also captivated.*

KING LEAR

Hast thou given all to thy two daughters?
And art thou come to this?

EDGAR

Who gives any thing to Poor Tom?
Bless thy five wits! Tom's a-cold,—O, do de, do de,
    do de.

KING LEAR

What, have his daughters brought him to this pass?
Couldst thou save nothing? Didst thou give them all?

EDGAR

Pillicock sat on Pillicock-hill:
Halloo, halloo, loo, loo!

EDGAR *moves stage right, flapping his arms like wings.*

FOOL

This cold night will turn us all to fools and madmen.

KING LEAR

> Is man no more than this? Unaccommodated man is
> no more but such a poor bare, forked animal as thou
> art.

FOOL *(looks stage left)*

> Look, here comes a walking fire.

Enter GLOUCESTER *from stage left, with a torch. He comes
to center stage. The men form a line from stage right to left:*
EDGAR, KING LEAR, GLOUCESTER, KENT, *and the* FOOL.

EDGAR

> This is the foul fiend Flibbertigibbet.

GLOUCESTER

> What are you there? Your names?

EDGAR

> Poor Tom, that in the fury of his heart, swallows
> the old rat and the ditch-dog; who is whipped from
> tithing to tithing! *(whips himself with his arms)*

GLOUCESTER

> What, hath your grace no better company?
> Go in with me: My duty cannot suffer
> To obey in all your daughters' hard commands.

KING LEAR *resists, moving stage right to converse silently with*
EDGAR. *He exchanges his crown for* EDGAR'S *hat.*

KENT

> Importune him once more to go, my lord;
> His wits begin to unsettle.

GLOUCESTER
> Canst thou blame him?
> His daughters seek his death: Ah, that good Kent!
> He said it would be thus, poor banish'd man!
> Thou say'st the king grows mad; I'll tell thee, friend,
> I am almost mad myself: I had a son,
> Now outlaw'd from my blood; he sought my life,
> But lately, very late: I loved him, friend,
> The grief hath crazed my wits.
> > *(motions for all to exit)*

KING LEAR
> O, cry your mercy, sir.
> Noble philosopher, your company.
> Come, good Athenian.

GLOUCESTER
> No words, no words: Hush.

Exit GLOUCESTER *stage right, leading* KING LEAR *off.* KENT *follows, while* EDGAR *remains.*

EDGAR
> Child Rowland to the dark tower came,
> His word was still,—Fie, foh, and fum,
> I smell the blood of a British man.

Exit EDGAR *stage right.*

✳ *KING LEAR:* PERFORMANCE NOTES

I directed this performance of *King Lear* in 2007. We began our production with a throne in the center of a bare stage. This presented a visual metaphor for Lear himself, an isolated ruler. Actors' physical characteristics can illustrate their psychic traits, while set staging reflects the play's themes.

The actor playing the Fool in our show sprained his ankle the day before the performance and was limping with a cane, which offered the unexpected bonus of having the Fool's movement echo Lear's, since Lear also walked with a cane. Sometimes accidents lead to new and revealing staging ideas. Use them! Sometimes the more tragic the play, the bigger the laughs, especially when one has a Fool such as this eighteen-year-old student, a young man with no acting experience, but great enthusiasm and a strong sense of play.

This same twelfth-grade actor enjoyed portraying the Fool in different shades as the play progressed: at times mischievous, at other times caustic. Sometimes the Fool acted as if he were Lear's parent, and at other times he behaved like a little boy. The Fool is a complex role and the text can be interpreted in various ways. Each different portrayal sheds new light on this tricky individual. Shakespeare's characters have many dimensions. Explore not only the role's nuances, but the changes the character undergoes as the story progresses.

Actors have different ways of arriving at moments of stage truth. Some remember moments in their own lives where they experienced similar emotions. Others approach the challenge from a more technical angle, using stylized movements and speech patterns to arrive at their interpretation of character. Sometimes I suggest a few possible choices. The most important suggestion I can give is that you commit to the moment and try to be fully present onstage, paying attention to the reality you have created. In a sense, it is a kind of mindfulness, engaging the five senses so one is fully alive, and able to convey that vitality to an audience.

In the play's final scene, Lear had been frail, but he is somewhat rejuvenated by the love of his daughter Cordelia, and his desire to protect her. For an actor, this presents an interesting dynamic: how to project strength within a context of physical weakness. Actors who are generally physically strong play these roles. When playing someone old and frail, performers must focus on achieving a consistent physical portrayal of one less hearty than themselves. If Lear has been shuffling with a cane since the first scene, he must shuffle with a cane in the last scene. Even if his frailty momentarily vanishes, as when he tries to protect his daughter, it must return promptly.

When we make strong physical choices in a production, it gives the other characters something to react to, which in turn elicits physicality from them. How the characters react to these actions tells us something about their personalities and relationships. Blocking choices like this help audiences sort out key plot and role details, allowing them to follow the story and become emotionally involved with the characters. Powerful blocking and stage pictures help us tell the story to the audience with clarity and feeling.

KING LEAR: ACT III, SCENE IV

At the beginning of this scene (Act III, Scene IV), Kent leads Lear onto the stage, protecting him from the storm. Then when the Fool runs out of the hovel, he cowers behind Lear, who puts his arm around the Fool protectively. The actors can use body language such as hunching over and wrapping cloaks around themselves to depict stormy weather. Additionally, prerecorded storm and rain sounds enhance the feeling of being out in nasty weather. Actors should continue to react physically to the storm throughout the scene. Loud, well-placed thunderclaps give them something they can react to. This scene is a good opportunity for players to use their bodies to depict a weather event: They should raise their voices to be heard over the storm and wind.

The Fool disappears in the middle of the scene, and Lear and Poor Tom stand stage right while Gloucester and Kent discuss Lear's condition. Lear and Poor Tom exchange headgear, so Lear is now wearing Poor Tom's hat and Poor Tom is wearing Lear's crown. It is as if Poor Tom has now replaced the Fool as Lear's shadow. These pieces of stage business emerge out of the rehearsal process. Each time an actor makes a choice, he is painting the character and relationships with his own brush.

When an actor makes a choice, it is helpful to discuss the reasons behind it, and the effect this acting decision has on the play. Why does Lear exchange hats with Poor Tom? Is it to show he is losing his grip on reality? Or is it so that he can, as Lear puts it, "feel what wretches feel"? Often the text itself will provide clues and cues upon which actors can base their choices. Encourage performers to mine the text carefully, because Shakespeare's words offer a treasure trove of staging possibilities.

Through their commitment to their scenes, the actors succeeded in transporting the audience into the world Shakespeare created for us. That is the magic of theater. *King Lear* is a towering and complex tragedy. I was very proud of this group of twelfth graders from a D.C. public school English class for bringing the play so compellingly to life. May this be your experience, too.

✳ *KING LEAR:* MONOLOGUE NOTES

ACT III, SCENE IV: KING LEAR MONOLOGUE

Shortly before this scene takes place, in Act III, Scene II of the play, King Lear says these words: "My wits begin to turn." Now, in the midst of a roaring storm, Lear is heading toward madness. However, he does not appear to be there yet. In this passage, King Lear directly addresses the possibility that he is going insane. Before he does so, though, he explains to Kent that the physical force of the storm on his body is nothing compared to the storm in his mind.

Here you have a choice of how to play Lear: lucid, going mad, or fully mad. Examine the text to see how it informs your acting choices. In his first six lines, Lear tells Kent, "Where the greater malady is fixed, the lesser is scarce felt." The metaphor that follows provides descriptive images of a bear on one side and a roaring sea on the other.

As the performer, you can make a physical gesture to depict the dynamic of being in between two punishing choices—"the roaring sea" and "a bear"—by acting out either the part of the bear or that of the person facing the bear. You can also depict the roaring sea with arm and hand motions or perhaps vocal sound effects. At any point during a descriptive line, you will make choices. Is Lear speaking directly to Kent? Is he addressing Kent implicitly but looking toward the audience? Is he speaking to himself?

The rhythm changes with the next set of lines. Up until the words "mind's free," the lines of the monologue are written in iambic pentameter. Whenever the rhythm and structure of the text changes, take the opportunity to alter the mood, take a breath, pause, and adjust vocal timbre, facial expression, and physical demeanor to reflect this change:

> *When the*
> *mind's free,*
> *The body's delicate.*

This line distills the monologue to its essence: Lear's tumultuous thoughts have lessened the storm's effect on his body. The words "mind," "free," "body's," and "delicate" each offer opportunities to experiment with word coloring, facial expression, and gesture. Try using differing attitudes. The line could be spoken with strength and defiance or with vulnerability. Lear could be having a personal revelation at this moment, or he could be explaining to Kent why his psychic turmoil overshadows the wind and rain.

Try putting the emphasis on the word "mind" and then switch the emphasis to the word "free." Does the shift in emphasis change the meaning of the phrase? Where is Lear's gaze? Is it directly on Kent? Toward the audience? Heavenward? By experimenting with different emotional, intellectual, and physical interpretations of the text, you'll reap great theatrical riches. Try the monologue in different ways, and your own performance will emerge.

When Lear exclaims "Filial ingratitude!" this could be the beginning of part three of the monologue, which pinpoints the source of the "tempest" in Lear's mind. Part one offers a metaphor and introductory explanation of the king's premise concerning inner versus outer turmoil. Part two, beginning with "When the mind's free," distills the idea into a coherent statement. Part three then describes the "inner tempest": Lear's fractured relationship with his daughters.

In part three, Lear addresses daughters Regan and Goneril by name. What do those names mean to him? This can be expressed vocally as well as physically. The performer may experiment with mood shifts. Perhaps the phrases ending in question marks could be played plaintively, almost wailing, whereas the answers—"But I will punish home," "Pour on," "I will endure"—have a defiant and fighting quality.

Lear's mind is now torn between strength and despair. Ultimately, he wrestles with himself, realizing that if he continues with his wrenching regrets, he may indeed go mad: "O, that way madness lies. Let me shun that; No more of that."

On these final lines, Lear can physically wrench himself away from that train of thought, as if the thoughts themselves had a physical hold on him. His voice might become lower and quieter as he talks to himself, trying to avoid slipping away from his own sanity. This passage represents different sides of King Lear: the powerful and the pathetic, the reasoning and the irrational. The monologue gives actors a great deal of material to work with, and by mining the text for its possibilities, you can deliver a powerful and moving piece of theatre.

SUGGESTED VIEWING

KING LEAR, 1983
Director: Michael Elliot
Starring: Laurence Olivier

KING LEAR, 2008
Director: Trevor Nunn
Starring: Ian McKellan

✳ LOVE'S LABOR'S LOST

CHARACTERS IN THE PLAY

The following is a list of characters that appear in this scene of Love's Labor's Lost.

THE PRINCESS OF FRANCE

ROSALINE

MARIA | Ladies attending on the Princess

KATHARINE

BOYET
| Lords attending on the Princess
MARCADE

KING FERDINAND: King of Navarre

BEROWNE

LONGAVILLE | Lords attending on the King

DUMAINE

SIR NATHANIEL: A curate

HOLOFERNES: A schoolmaster

COSTARD: A clown

DON ARMADO: A fantastical Spaniard

MOTH: Page to Don Armado

NARRATOR

SET AND PROP LIST

SET PIECES:
Table
Two benches
Throne

PROPS:
Jewels for Princess
Letter and earrings for Rosaline
Gloves and letter for Katharine
Pearls and letter for Maria
Masks or veils for Ladies
Russian habits and masks for the Lords
Shields, helmets, swords, axes for the Worthies

✳ *LOVE'S LABOR'S LOST:* ACT V, SCENE II

Before the Princess's pavilion.

Enter NARRATOR *from stage rear, coming downstage.*

NARRATOR

> The king and his lords, disguised as Russians, visit
> the ladies, who have their fun by confusing the men.
> Poor misguided men! How will it all end?

Exit NARRATOR *stage right.*

Enter the PRINCESS, KATHARINE, ROSALINE, *and* MARIA *from
stage rear. The* PRINCESS *and* KATHARINE *stand in front of stage
right bench;* ROSALINE *and* MARIA *stand in front of stage left
bench.*

PRINCESS

> Sweet hearts, we shall be rich ere we depart,
> If fairings come thus plentifully in.
> A lady wall'd about with diamonds! *(displays
>   her jewels)*
> Look you what I have from the loving king.
> But, Rosaline, you have a favor too:
> Who sent it? And what is it?

ROSALINE

> I thank Berowne;
> I am compar'd to twenty thousand fairs.
> O! He hath drawn my picture in his letter.
>   *(displays a letter and earrings)*

PRINCESS

But, Katharine, what was sent to you from
fair Dumaine?

KATHARINE

Madam, this glove.

PRINCESS

Did he not send you twain?

KATHARINE

Yes, madam; and, moreover,
Some thousand verses of a faithful lover;
(displays gloves and a letter)
A huge translation of hypocrisy,
Vilely compil'd, profound simplicity.

MARIA

This, and these pearl, to me sent Longaville;
(displays pearls and a letter)
The letter is too long by half a mile.

PRINCESS

I think no less. Dost thou not wish in heart
The chain were longer and the letter short?

MARIA

Ay, or I would these hands might never part.

PRINCESS

We are wise girls to mock our lovers so.

ROSALINE

They are worse fools to purchase mocking so.
That same Berowne I'll torture ere I go.

O that I knew he were but in by th' week!
How I would make him fawn, and beg, and seek.

PRINCESS

None are so surely caught, when they are catch'd,
As wit turn'd fool: Folly, in wisdom hatch'd,
Hath wisdom's warrant and the help of school
And wit's own grace to grace a learned fool.

Enter BOYET *from stage rear.*

PRINCESS

Here comes Boyet, and mirth is in his face. *(stands)*

BOYET

O! I am stabb'd with laughter! Where's her Grace?

PRINCESS

Thy news, Boyet?

BOYET

Prepare, madam, prepare! Love doth approach
        disguised,
Armed in arguments; you'll be surpris'd.

PRINCESS

But what, but what, come they to visit us?

BOYET

They do, they do, and are apparell'd thus,
Like Muscovites or Russians, as I guess.
Their purpose is to parley, court, and dance;
And every one his love-feat will advance
Unto his several mistress; which they'll know
By favors several which they did bestow.

PRINCESS
>And will they so? The gallants shall be task'd:
>For, ladies, we will every one be mask'd;
>Hold, Rosaline, this favor thou shalt wear,
>>*(gives* ROSALINE *her jewels)*
>And then the king will court thee for his dear;
>Hold, take thou this, my sweet, and give me thine,
>>*(*ROSALINE *gives the* PRINCESS *her earrings)*
>So shall Berowne take me for Rosaline.
>And change you favors too; so shall your loves
>Woo contrary, deceiv'd by these removes.
>>*(*MARIA *gives* KATHARINE *her pearl necklace;*
>>KATHARINE *gives* MARIA *her gloves)*
>The effect of my intent is to cross theirs;
>They do it but in mocking merriment;
>And mock for mock is only my intent.
>So shall we stay, mocking intended game,
>And they well mock'd, depart away with shame.

SOUND OPERATOR *plays* Sound Cue #1 ("Trumpet sounds").

BOYET
>The trumpet sounds: Be mask'd; the maskers come.

The LADIES *put their veils over their faces.*

Enter MOTH, FERDINAND, BEROWNE, LONGAVILLE, *and* DUMAINE, *dressed in Russian habits and wearing masks.*

MOTH
>"All hail, the richest beauties on the earth!"
>>*(unsure of which masked lady to talk to)*
>A holy parcel of the fairest dames

The LADIES *turn their backs to him.*

That ever turn'd their—backs—to mortal views!

BEROWNE
"Their eyes," villain, "their eyes."

MOTH
"That ever turn'd their eyes to mortal views!"

BEROWNE
Is this your perfectness? Be gone, you rogue.

Exit MOTH *stage right.*

ROSALINE *(as* PRINCESS*)*
What would these strangers? Know their minds,
Boyet.

BOYET
What would you with the princess?

BEROWNE
Nothing but peace and gentle visitation.

ROSALINE
What would they, say they?

BOYET
Nothing but peace and gentle visitation.

ROSALINE
Why, that they have; and bid them so be gone.

BOYET
She says you have it, and you may be gone.

FERDINAND
>Say to her we have measur'd many miles
>To tread a measure with her on this grass.

SOUND OPERATOR *plays* Sound Cue # 2 ("Dance music").

FERDINAND *goes to* **ROSALINE**, *who is sitting on downstage side of stage right bench; he offers his hand to dance but she does not return her hand.*

FERDINAND
>Will you not dance? How come you thus estranged?

ROSALINE
>You took the moon at full; but now she's chang'd.

FERDINAND *and* **ROSALINE** *freeze.*

BEROWNE *(goes to the* **PRINCESS**, *who is sitting on downstage side of stage left bench)*
>White-handed mistress, one sweet word with thee.

PRINCESS
>Honey, and milk, and sugar; there is three.

BEROWNE *and the* **PRINCESS** *freeze.*

DUMAINE *(goes to* **MARIA**, *who is sitting on upstage side of stage right bench)*
>Will you vouchsafe with me to change a word?

MARIA
>Name it.

DUMAINE
>Fair lady,—

MARIA

Say you so? Fair lord,
Take that for your fair lady.

DUMAINE *and* MARIA *freeze.*

LONGAVILLE *goes to* KATHERINE *who is sitting on upstage side of stage left bench.*

KATHARINE

What, was your vizard made without a tongue?

LONGAVILLE

You have a double tongue within your mask,
And would afford my speechless vizard half.
One word in private with you ere I die.

KATHARINE

Bleat softly, then; the butcher hears you cry.

KATHARINE *and* LONGAVILLE *freeze.*

ROSALINE *(unfreezes, along with* FERDINAND)

Not one word more, my maids; break off, break off.

The rest unfreeze.

BEROWNE

By heaven, all dry-beaten with pure scoff!

FERDINAND

Farewell, mad wenches; you have simple wits.

PRINCESS

Twenty adieus, my frozen Muscovits.

Exit FERDINAND *and his* LORDS *stage right.*

The LADIES *come to center stage together, laughing.*

ROSALINE

> O! They were all in lamentable cases!
> The King was weeping-ripe for a good word.

PRINCESS

> Berowne did swear himself out of all suit.

MARIA

> Dumaine was at my service, and his sword:
> "No point" quoth I; my servant straight was mute.

KATHARINE

> Lord Longaville said, I came o'er his heart.

BOYET *(from stage right)*

> Madam, and pretty mistresses, give ear:
> Immediately they will again be here
> In their own shapes.

ROSALINE

> Good madam, if by me you'll be advis'd,
> Let's mock them still, as well known as disguis'd.
> Let us complain to them what fools were here,
> Disguis'd like Muscovites, in shapeless gear.

BOYET

> Ladies, withdraw: The gallants are at hand.

The PRINCESS, ROSALINE, KATHARINE, *and* MARIA *hide behind stage left pillar.*

Enter FERDINAND, BEROWNE, LONGAVILLE, *and* DUMAINE *in their proper habits from stage right.*

FERDINAND

Fair sir, God save you! Where's the princess?

BOYET

Gone to her tent.

The **PRINCESS, ROSALINE, MARIA,** *and* **KATHARINE** *come out from behind stage left pillar; the* **PRINCESS** *greets* **FERDINAND** *center stage as the other ladies return to their original positions in front of benches.*

FERDINAND

All hail, sweet madam, and fair time of day!

PRINCESS

We have had pastimes here, and pleasant game.
A mess of Russians left us but of late.

FERDINAND

How, madam! Russians?

PRINCESS

Ay, in truth, my lord;
Trim gallants, full of courtship and of state.
(looks at **FERDINAND** *knowingly)*
Were not you here but even now, disguis'd?

FERDINAND *(confessing)*

Madam, I was.

PRINCESS

Rosaline, what did the Russian whisper in your ear?

ROSALINE

Madam, he swore that he did hold me dear
Adding that he would wed me, or else die my lover.

PRINCESS

> The noble lord
> Most honorably doth uphold his word.

FERDINAND

> What mean you, madam? By my life, my troth,
> I never swore this lady such an oath.

ROSALINE

> By heaven, you did; and, to confirm it plain,
> You gave me this: But take it, sir, again.

FERDINAND

> My faith and this the princess I did give;
> I knew her by this jewel on her sleeve.

PRINCESS

> Pardon me, sir, this jewel did she wear;
> And Lord Berowne, I thank him, is my dear.

BEROWNE

> I see the trick on't: Here was a consent,
> Knowing aforehand of our merriment,
> To dash it like a Christmas comedy.
> The ladies did change favors, and then we,
> Following the signs, woo'd but the sign of she.
> Now, to our perjury to add more terror,
> We are again forsworn, in will and error.

Enter COSTARD *from stage rear.*

> Welcome, pure wit! Thou part'st a fair fray.

COSTARD

> O Lord, sir, they would know
> Whether the three Worthies shall come in or no?

BEROWNE

Go, bid them prepare.

Exit COSTARD *stage rear.*

FERDINAND

The ship is under sail, and here she comes amain.

The four men and four women sit as couples on the benches, to watch the show.

Enter COSTARD *from stage rear, to perform "Pompey."*

COSTARD

"I Pompey am"—
That oft in field, with targe and shield, did make
my foe to sweat:
And travelling along this coast, I here am come
by chance,
And lay my arms before the legs of this sweet lass
of France.

BEROWNE

Pompey proves the best Worthy.

Enter SIR NATHANIEL *from stage rear, to perform "Alexander."*

SIR NATHANIEL

"When in the world I liv'd, I was the world's
commander;
By east, west, north, and south, I spread my
conquering might:
My scutcheon plain declares that I am Alisander"—

BEROWNE
Pompey the Great,—
Take away the conqueror, take away Alisander.

COSTARD (*to* SIR NATHANIEL)
Run away for shame, Alisander.

Exit SIR NATHANIEL *stage right.*

But there are Worthies a-coming will speak their
mind in some other sort.

PRINCESS
Stand aside, good Pompey.

Enter HOLOFERNES *and* MOTH *from stage rear, to perform "Judas" and "Hercules," respectively.* MOTH *stands to* HOLOFERNES'S *left.*

HOLOFERNES
"Great Hercules is presented by this imp,
Whose club kill'd Cerberus, that three-headed canis;
And when he was a babe, a child, a shrimp,
Thus did he strangle serpents in his manus.
Keep some state in thy exit, and vanish.— "

Exit MOTH *stage left.*

HOLOFERNES (stands center stage, declaiming)
"Judas I am."—

DUMAINE
A Judas!

HOLOFERNES

Not Iscariot, sir.

"Judas I am, ycliped Maccabaeus."

DUMAINE

Judas Maccabaeus clipt is plain Judas.

BOYET

Therefore, as he is an ass, let him go.

And so adieu, sweet Jude! Nay, why dost thou stay?

DUMAINE

For the latter end of his name.

BEROWNE

For the ass to the Jude? Give it him: Jud as, away!

HOLOFERNES

This is not generous, not gentle, not humble.

Exit HOLOFERNES *stage right.*

PRINCESS

Alas! Poor Maccabaeus, how hath he been baited.

Enter ARMADO, *coming stage right to perform "Hector."*

BEROWNE

Hide thy head, Achilles: Here comes Hector in arms.

ARMADO

"The armipotent Mars, of lances the almighty,

Gave Hector a gift, the heir of Ilion;

A man so breath'd that certain he would fight ye,

From morn till night, out of his pavilion.

I am that flower,"—

DUMAINE

> That mint.

LONGAVILLE

> That columbine.

ARMADO

> Sweet Lord Longaville, rein thy tongue.
> I will forward with my device. *(draws his sword
>   toward* COSTARD, *who is stage left)*
> By the north pole, I do challenge thee.

COSTARD

> I'll slash; I'll do it by the sword.
> I bepray you, let me borrow my arms again.

DUMAINE

> Room for the incensed Worthies!

COSTARD

> I'll do it in my shirt.

DUMAINE

> Most resolute Pompey hath made the challenge!

ARMADO

> Sweet bloods, I both may and will.

ARMADO *and* COSTARD *are about to fight, and* MOTH *is trying to separate them.*

Enter MONSIEUR MARCADE, *a messenger, from stage rear.*

MARCADE

> God save you, madam!

PRINCESS
> Welcome, Marcade;
> But that thou interrupt'st our merriment.

MARCADE
> I am sorry, madam; for the news I bring
> Is heavy in my tongue. The king your father—

PRINCESS
> Dead, for my life!

MARCADE
> Even so: My tale is told.

BEROWNE
> Worthies away! The scene begins to cloud.

First MOTH, *then* COSTARD, *then* ARMADO *exit, but* ARMADO *turns before exiting.*

ARMADO
> For mine own part, I breathe free breath.

Exit ARMADO.

FERDINAND *(bowing his head, wishing to comfort the* PRINCESS
> *but not feeling bold enough)*
> How fares your Majesty?

PRINCESS *(in mourning)*
> Boyet, prepare: I will away to-night.

FERDINAND
> Madam, not so: I do beseech you stay.

PRINCESS
> Farewell, worthy lord!
> A heavy heart bears not a nimble tongue.

BEROWNE *(stepping forward)*
> Honest plain words best pierce the ear of grief;
> For your fair sakes have we play'd foul play with
>   our oaths.
> Your beauty, ladies,
> Hath much deform'd us, fashioning our humors
> Even to the opposed end of our intents.

PRINCESS
> We have receiv'd your letters, full of love;
> Your favors, the ambassadors of love;
> And, in our maiden council, rated them
> At courtship, pleasant jest, and courtesy,
> and therefore met your loves
> In their own fashion, like a merriment.

DUMAINE
> Our letters, madam, show'd much more than jest.

LONGAVILLE
> So did our looks.

ROSALINE
> We did not quote them so.

FERDINAND
> Now, at the latest minute of the hour,
> Grant us your loves.

PRINCESS *(to* FERDINAND*)*

 A time, methinks, too short
 To make a world-without-end bargain in.
 No, no, my lord, your Grace is perjured much,
 Full of dear guiltiness, and therefore this:
 If for my love—as there is no such cause—
 You will do aught, this shall you do for me:
 Your oath I will not trust, but go with speed
 To some forlorn and naked hermitage,
 Remote from all the pleasures of the world.
 There stay until the twelve celestial signs
 Have brought about the annual reckoning.
 If this austere insociable life
 Change not your offer made in heat of blood;
 If frosts and fasts, hard lodging, and thin weeds
 Nip not the gaudy blossoms of your love,
 But that it bear this trial, and last love;
 Then, at the expiration of the year,
 Come challenge me, challenge me by these deserts,

PRINCESS *takes* FERDINAND'S *hand.*

 And by this virgin palm now kissing thine,
 I will be thine. And till that instant shut
 My woeful self up in a mourning house,
 Raining the tears of lamentation
 For the remembrance of my father's death.
 If this thou do deny, let our hands part,
 Neither entitled in the other's heart.

FERDINAND

 Hence hermit, then. My heart is in thy breast.

DUMAINE *(to* KATHARINE*)*

 But what to me, my love? But what to me?

KATHARINE
> Come when the King doth to my lady come;
> Then, if I have much love, I'll give you some.

DUMAINE
> I'll serve thee true and faithfully till then.

KATHARINE
> Yet swear not, lest ye be forsworn again.

LONGAVILLE *(to* MARIA*)*
> What says Maria?

MARIA
> At the twelvemonth's end
> I'll change my black gown for a faithful friend.

LONGAVILLE
> I'll stay with patience; but the time is long.

BEROWNE *(to* ROSALINE*)*
> Mistress, look on me;
> Impose some service on me for thy love.

ROSALINE
> My lord Berowne,
> You shall this twelvemonth term, from day to day,
> Visit the speechless sick, and still converse
> With groaning wretches; and your task shall be,
> With all the fierce endeavour of your wit
> To enforce the pained impotent to smile.
> A jest's prosperity lies in the ear
> Of him that hears it, never in the tongue
> Of him that makes it.

BEROWNE

A twelvemonth! Well, befall what will befall,
I'll jest a twelvemonth in an hospital.

PRINCESS *(to* FERDINAND*)*

Ay, sweet my lord; and so I take my leave.

FERDINAND

No, madam; we will bring you on your way.

The PRINCESS *shakes her head no.*

BEROWNE

Our wooing doth not end like an old play:
Jack hath not Jill; these ladies' courtesy
Might well have made our sport a comedy.

FERDINAND

Come, sir, it wants a twelvemonth and a day,
And then 'twill end.

BEROWNE

That's too long for a play.

Enter ARMADO *from stage rear.*

ARMADO

Sweet Majesty, vouchsafe me—Will you hear the
dialogue that the two learned men have compiled
in praise of the owl and the cuckoo? It should have
followed in the end of our show.

FERDINAND

Call them forth quickly; we will do so.

ARMADO

Holla! Approach.

Enter HOLOFERNES, NATHANIEL, MOTH, COSTARD, *and others from stage rear.*

This is Hiems, Winter; maintained by the owl,
Ver, begin.

ALL *(standing in a line with a simple right/left step and reciting together)*
When all aloud the wind doth blow,
And coughing drowns the parson's saw,
And birds sit brooding in the snow,
And Marian's nose looks red and raw,
When roasted crabs hiss in the bowl,
Then nightly sings the staring owl:
Tu-who;
Tu-whit, to-who—a merry note,
While greasy Joan doth keel the pot.

ARMADO

The words of Mercury are harsh after the songs
of Apollo.
(to audience) You that way: *(gestures to self and cast)*
We this way.

ALL *hold hands and take a bow. Exeunt.*

✳ *LOVE'S LABOR'S LOST:* PERFORMANCE NOTES

I directed this version of *Love's Labor's Lost* in 2003 with a group of ninth graders. The young cast had a great time with the courtship, the mistaken identity, the silly Russian dances, and the play-within-a-play, "The Nine Worthies." The characters are colorful and the language is rich. The play is merry, but it also has a serious side, and it is one of the few Shakespearean comedies not to end in happy marriages. I like comedies that have a serious flip side. The contrast allows you to express range and dynamics.

This cast of ninth graders was responsive, committed, and enthusiastic, but they had one problematic quality that I failed to reign in by show day: They spoke too fast. Many actors deliver their lines too quickly, which can confuse the audience. Finding beats and breathing points in the script helps control this tendency. Mark a slash in your texts at appropriate breathing points. Underline emphasized words or syllables, and experiment with changing the emphasis to hear how the line's meaning changes as well. Practice "coloring" the words—think of the word as something to evoke emotion, instead of just a word. See if the word can become a poem in itself, with richness that echoes its sentiment, or if it can enhance the image it arouses. This exercise will encourage you to slow down your speech and allow the words to breathe and convey their fullest meaning.

Additionally, actors need to modulate their voices. It is helpful to compare the text to a song. Players can sing their lines to experiment with variations in pitch and tempo. They can also try saying their parts like a TV newscaster, an opera singer, or a grizzly bear.

Animal imagery can be a good way to encourage actors to explore their characters' animal essences. Actors must practice diction exercises too, such as tongue twisters, and bouncing off consonants. Use these exercises in rehearsal to expand the performers' vocal range.

Actors should pick up very quickly on each other's cues, allowing the dialogue to bounce back and forth between them like a ping-pong game, but they must still speak at a moderate pace for the sake of comprehension. The best way to tighten up quick exchanges of this kind is to practice picking up on each other's cues in rehearsal. Actors often memorize their lines, but forget to memorize the cues that come before them. Memorize cues too!

Love's Labor's Lost features many merry moments in which the focus shifts back and forth swiftly between players in snappy repartee. Precise blocking and timing are therefore essential to the success of the comedy. Once the blocking is rehearsed and finalized, players can loosen up and have fun within the context of choreographed conversations. In this sense the play is like a dance. In fact, enlisting the assistance of a dance instructor is always a good idea. Outside instructors in dance, music, voice, and other disciplines bring a fresh perspective and can provide exciting instruction and suggestions.

One person having a lot of fun on stage is often all it takes to bring cast members and the audience along. If nobody is having fun, it is your job to get the ball rolling. Laughter and merriment are contagious. Bring your love of theatre and Shakespeare into the rehearsal process and joy will follow. In our production, the performer playing the Princess had an enthusiasm for her character that carried the other actors along with her, which helped to clearly advance the plot, but more importantly, furthered the fun.

The structure of the action and dialogue in *Love's Labor's Lost* allows for the technique of freezing the action so that the audience's eyes focus on one couple at a time. When one couple is on the bench, for example, all other actors freeze while facing in their direction, creating the impression that the wooers have stepped out of time into their own world. This is a great way to give complete focus over to one couple at a time.

To enhance the verbal back and forth between Rosaline and Berowne, we designed physical moves to accompany the dialogue: In one scene, as Berowne brought his arm around Rosaline, she stood up rapidly, causing Berowne to fall onto the bench. Berowne then stood quickly, and returned to Rosaline's side. The words provoke a movement. That movement causes a physical response, which in turn elicits commentary, and so on. It is a dance.

LOVE'S LABOR'S LOST: ACT V, SCENE II

I can't emphasize enough how important it is for actors to make their own choices to portray a character. Having said that, there is nothing wrong with suggesting a number of possibilities. Actors need direction, but once they are in motion, their natural personality and talents emerge, and they bring their own magic to a scene.

The narrator in Act V, Scene II has the line "How will it all end?" After delivering the question, she skipped offstage merrily. This was her choice, and I imagine she did it just for fun once in rehearsal, and I urged her to keep it. I would not want a narrator to skip off stage in *King Lear*. But this is *Love's Labor's Lost*. The actress successfully absorbed and reflected the lighthearted mood of the play.

The "Russians" enter this scene wearing Fez hats, dark goatees, and ridiculously glued-on black bushy false eyebrows: a nice touch! Gypsy dance music plays and the four performers commence a high-stepping, leg-kicking Cossack dance with tassels flying off their hats. The audience claps loudly in rhythm, and to end the dance, the Russians throw their arms upward in tight unison and let out an exuberant cry of "Woo!" The audience erupted in approving applause.

When there is a moment in a comedy where over-the-top silliness, music, dancing, and goofy costumes are called for, don't hold back. Exaggerate the comedy past the point that you might be comfortable. Trust this advice, because it will pay off. It's worth a try!

We employed the freezing technique again in this scene, in keeping with the notion that pieces of stage business are best repeated if possible, to develop a movement language for your production. After each man wooed his respective woman, the couples froze two by two, until all actors were frozen for a brief moment. Then Rosaline and King unfroze, and when Rosaline said, "break off," all unfroze.

This production of *Love's Labor's Lost* closes with the comical play-within-a-play, "The Nine Worthies." This gives us another opportunity for silly costuming. Our 2003 performance featured plastic-horned, fur-trimmed Viking helmets, gaudily adorned plastic shields, and wooden swords. These are good outfits in which to strike exaggerated, silly poses.

When Pompey enters and exclaims, "and lay my arms before the legs of this sweet lass of France," he mistakenly kneels at Berowne's feet, and Berowne points across the stage toward the Princess, setting a jocular tone for the scene.

The actor playing Dumaine took great pleasure in calling Holofernes "Jude-ass" instead of "Judas," as a setup to the subsequent puns on the word "ass." Shakespeare's bawdy and risqué wordplay holds a special appeal for audiences. Do not shy away from exploiting these "naughty" double entendres. Actors and audiences delight in them.

We finish "The Nine Worthies" with an effective tableau: Moth stands between Armado and Costard, keeping them apart with a sword in one hand and an axe in the other. This particular version of *Love's Labor's Lost,* with the aid of the freezing technique, makes excellent use of visual tableaux. Once we establish a theatrical vocabulary, we use repetition of staging methods to create a production that has visual and dramatic unity.

The merry revelry of "The Nine Worthies" comes to a crashing halt with the announcement of the death of Princess's father. At play's end, each couple rises from their seats in sequence to determine the future of their relationship, and each is told to wait a year and a day, leaving us with a lack of dramatic closure unusual for a Shakespearean comedy.

What better way to end *Love's Labor's Lost* than with the cast reciting The Winter Poem in unison, swaying gently as a group from side to side? A pair of onstage cast members should start the group recitation as other cast members come onstage so as to preempt premature audience applause. In the 2003 performance, the actors' voices rose buoyantly into the high registers on "to whoo!" and my spirit rose with them.

Armado announces to the audience, "You that way," and then gestures to himself and the cast, "We this way," and we all travel the way of joy, in the performance of a Shakespeare play. *Love's Labor's Lost* is a colorful and enchanting comedy. Using this book as a guideline, I hope that the experience of performing this show will bring delight and laughter to both actors and audiences alike.

✳ *LOVE'S LABOR'S LOST:* MONOLOGUE NOTES

ACT V, SCENE II: PRINCESS MONOLOGUE

This speech comes on the heels of the announcement that the Princess's father, the King of France, has died. The monologue is informed at all times by the emotional impact of this recent news. It is necessarily a sad passage. Within the mournful words, though, there is a promise of love. Play this speech with that hope in mind. Since the Princess and the women have just spent a merry and jesting time with the men, do not lose all the momentum of the joyful interactions that come before this more somber speech. In this monologue, as with other speeches, the more you know about your character's words and actions through-out the play, the better informed you will be on how to play a specific soliloquy. In other words, despite the sad tidings and the Princess's sorrowful words, be sure to play both her core of happiness as well as the practicality and intelligence she has exhibited thus far.

The Princess's first line is in response to the King of Navarre's words: "Now, at the latest minute of the hour, grant us your loves." If you are performing this scene with another actor playing the King, you may start with this line and proceed with the speech as writ-ten. If you are playing the piece as a solo monologue, you will have to choose where to start. Since the Princess's first sentence refers to what the King has just said, it does not make sense to start there, nor does it sound right to begin with "No, no." Therefore, if performing the speech alone, I suggest starting with, "My lord, your Grace is perjured much . . ."

The Princess starts by directly addressing the King's "dear guilti-ness." The notes to the Folger Shakespeare Library edition of *Love's Labor's Lost* define "dear" in this line as meaning 1) dire and/or 2) endearing. Perhaps you can play both meanings; in chiding the King for breaking his vow to retire from the world of women, the Princess still displays affection for him, seeing his good aspects through his faults. There might be a hint of playfulness in her voice as she says "dear guiltiness." A brief sparkle could even show through the sadness in her eyes.

The Princess's cautious nature reveals itself through her words, "Your oath I will not trust." The next few lines paint a bleak picture by using adjectives such as "forlorn," "remote," "austere," and "insocia-ble." You can color particular words such as "forlorn" by considering the Princess's emotional state of mourning. Draw the vowels out on "forlorn" and let them depict her heartbreak. Likewise, when she says "remote from all the pleasures of the world," this can again be a description of her own feelings. Maybe her voice breaks here to indi-cate emotion. Now that she is fatherless, the loneliness the Princess describes for the Prince might also be her own.

Starting with "If this austere insociable life," the Princess's cou-plets contrast the cold environment she envisions for the Prince with the heat of his passion. When she describes the Prince's "heat of blood," this might ignite her own heart as she gazes directly into his eyes with a touch of intensity. Throughout this passage, hope pushes through sorrow, hot blood warms cold skin, and love fends off loneli-ness. Accentuate the hard consonants on these descriptive nouns— "frosts," "fasts," "hard," "thin," and "weeds"—to paint a bitter picture with your words. Then open up the sensuous vowels on "gaudy," "blossoms," and "love" and let the possibility of romance soothe the Princess's aching heart.

The Princess makes an exhortation, and repeats it for emphasis: "Come challenge me, challenge me by these deserts." This is the most passionate, yearning, and hopeful sentence in the speech. Try utter-ing it softly and romantically with a gentle tone. Then try the line again with a bit more ferocity and command. Finally, try it a third time with desperation. Experimenting with levels of intensity on key passages can help your performance. Try rehearsing in front of a mirror or videotape yourself to see which approach you prefer. You will often end up choosing a nuanced interpretation such as gentle intensity.

The Princess now takes the King's hand. Following the "Challenge me" line, this can be a particularly poignant piece of stage business. If playing the monologue solo, you can place one hand flat in front of you and gently lay the other hand on top of it. Again, we have a word repetition: "thine." The first "thine" refers to the King's hand that the Princess touches with her own. The second "thine" suggests that this "kissing of palms" symbolizes a commitment that her heart will belong to the King. Try pausing slightly after "I will be . . ." and take one step closer to the King. The second "thine" will have greater impact if you wait a beat before speaking.

The monologue ends with the Princess returning to a state of mourning for her father. The passage weeps with sorrowful words one after another: "woeful," "mourning," "raining," "tears," and "lamentation." On the line "my father's death," the Princess's voice could crack with emotion as the finality of her father's passing strikes her. Recovering from that emotional moment, the Princess's practical, realistic side returns as she proposes her terms to the King. If he denies her proposal that he spend a year away from the comforts of the world, they will not be together.

Try the following physical gesture to close the speech. On the words "remembrance of my father's death," clasp your hands in prayer. On "let our hands part," unclasp them, and with "in the other's heart," gently put your hands over your heart.

In the Princess of France, Shakespeare has created a strong female character who sometimes sees love as a merry occasion and at other times as deadly serious. In this poignant speech, express her powerful emotions by speaking Shakespeare's words thoughtfully and with feeling, moving from the cold frost of death to the fiery hope of love.

SUGGESTED VIEWING

LOVE'S LABOUR'S LOST, 1985
Director: *Elijah Moshinsky*
Starring: *Christopher Blake, Maureen Lippman*

LOVE'S LABOUR'S LOST, 2000
Director: *Kenneth Branagh*
Starring: *Allessandro Nivoloa, Alicia Silverstone*

✳ MACBETH

CHARACTERS IN THE PLAY

The following is a list of characters that appear in this scene of Macbeth.

MACBETH: A Scottish general, Thane of Glamis
LADY MACBETH: Macbeth's ambitious wife
NARRATOR

SET AND PROP LIST

SET PIECES:
Two chairs
Table

PROPS:
Letter for Lady Macbeth
Two daggers for Macbeth

* *MACBETH:* ACT I, SCENE V; ACT II, SCENES I AND II

Inverness, Macbeth's castle.

Enter **NARRATOR** *from stage left.*

NARRATOR
> Lady Macbeth reads her husband's letter about his meeting with the Witches. Macbeth arrives, and she tells him that she will take charge of the preparations for King Duncan's murder.

Exit **NARRATOR** *stage rear.*

Enter **LADY MACBETH** *from stage right, reading a letter. She sits in chair stage left.*

LADY MACBETH *(having read the letter)*
> Glamis thou art, and Cawdor, and shalt be
> What thou art promised. Yet do I fear thy nature;
> It is too full o' th' milk of human kindness
> To catch the nearest way. Thou wouldst be great,
> Art not without ambition, but without
> The illness should attend it. What thou wouldst highly,
> That wouldst thou holily; wouldst not play false
> And yet wouldst wrongly win. Thou'dst have,
>   great Glamis,
> That which cries "Thus thou must do," if thou have it,
> And that which rather thou dost fear to do,
> Than wishest should be undone. Hie thee hither,

That I may pour my spirits in thine ear
And chastise with the valor of my tongue
All that impedes thee from the golden round,
Which fate and metaphysical aid doth seem
To have thee crowned withal.

Enter MACBETH *from stage right.* LADY MACBETH *goes to greet him, excited to see him, and kisses his hand. She leads him to the chair downstage left.*

MACBETH *(not yet sitting, turns to her)*
My dearest love,
Duncan comes here to-night.

LADY MACBETH
And when goes hence?

MACBETH
To-morrow, as he purposes.

LADY MACBETH
O, never
Shall sun that morrow see!
Your face, my thane, is as a book where men
May read strange matters.
(sits MACBETH *in chair and looks at him)* Look like the
	innocent flower,
But be the serpent under't. He that's coming
Must be provided for: and you shall put
This night's great business into my dispatch;
Which shall to all our nights and days to come
Give solely sovereign sway and masterdom.

MACBETH
We will speak further.

LADY MACBETH
>Only look up clear;
>To alter favor ever is to fear:
>Leave all the rest to me.

Exit LADY MACBETH *stage rear.*

MACBETH *(still sitting in chair; sees dagger in front of him)*
>Is this a dagger which I see before me,
>The handle toward my hand? Come, let me clutch thee.
>>*(tries to clutch dagger, but it has no substance)*
>I have thee not, and yet I see thee still.
>Art thou not, fatal vision, sensible
>To feeling as to sight? Or art thou but
>A dagger of the mind, a false creation,
>Proceeding from the heat-oppressed brain?
>I see thee yet, in form as palpable
>As this which now I draw.
>>*(draws his own dagger from belt)*
>Thou marshall'st me the way that I was going;
>And such an instrument I was to use.
>Thou sure and firm-set earth,
>Hear not my steps, which way they walk, for fear
>Thy very stones prate of my whereabout.

SOUND OPERATOR *plays* Sound Cue #1 ("Bell ring").

>I go, and it is done; the bell invites me.
>Hear it not, Duncan; for it is a knell
>That summons thee to heaven or to hell.

Exit MACBETH *stage rear. Enter* LADY MACBETH *from stage left.*

LADY MACBETH
>That which hath made them drunk hath made
>>me bold;
>What hath quench'd them hath given me fire.

I have drugg'd their possets,
That death and nature do contend about them,
Whether they live or die.

SOUND OPERATOR *plays* Sound Cue #2 ("Shrieking owl").

Hark! Peace!
It was the owl that shriek'd,

Enter MACBETH *from stage rear. His hands are bloody and he holds two bloody daggers.*

My husband!

MACBETH
I have done the deed. Didst thou not hear a noise?

LADY MACBETH
I heard the owl scream and the crickets cry.

MACBETH *(looking at his hands)*
This is a sorry sight.

LADY MACBETH *(grabs him by the shoulders to calm him down)*
A foolish thought, to say a sorry sight.

MACBETH
Methought I heard a voice cry "Sleep no more!
Macbeth does murder sleep"—the innocent sleep,
Sleep that knits up the ravell'd sleeve of care,
"Macbeth shall sleep no more."

LADY MACBETH
Who was it that thus cried? Why, worthy thane,
You do unbend your noble strength, to think
So brainsickly of things. *(notices daggers)*

Why did you bring these daggers from the place?
They must lie there: Go carry them; and smear
The sleepy grooms with blood. *(pushes him back
toward door)*

MACBETH *(resists her pushing and becomes more agitated)*
I'll go no more:
I am afraid to think what I have done;
Look on't again I dare not.

LADY MACBETH
Infirm of purpose! *(takes daggers from him)*
Give me the daggers: The sleeping and the dead
Are but as pictures: 'Tis the eye of childhood
That fears a painted devil. If he do bleed,
I'll gild the faces of the grooms withal;
For it must seem their guilt.

Exit **LADY MACBETH** *stage rear.*

SOUND OPERATOR *plays* Sound Cue #3 ("Knocking").

MACBETH
Whence is that knocking?
How is't with me, when every noise appals me?
(looks at his hands)
What hands are here? Ha! They pluck out mine eyes.
Will all great Neptune's ocean wash this blood
Clean from my hand?

Re-enter **LADY MACBETH**.

LADY MACBETH
My hands are of your color; but I shame
To wear a heart so white.

SOUND OPERATOR *plays* Sound Cue #4 ("Knocking").

MACBETH

To know my deed, 'twere best not know myself.

SOUND OPERATOR *plays* Sound Cue #5 ("Knocking").

Wake Duncan with thy knocking! I would thou couldst!

Exit MACBETH *and* LADY MACBETH *stage left, hurriedly.*

✳ *MACBETH:* PERFORMANCE NOTES

For actors, there is a delicious joy in conjuring the evil that pervades *Macbeth*. Against a backdrop of "fog and filthy air," the play not only gives us a wealth of bloody deeds, but also their psychic consequences. This excerpt from "The Scottish Play" offers us an opportunity to mine Shakespeare's text for all the poetic horror it offers. Once you have played in *Macbeth,* you may never be the same again.

I directed this performance of *Macbeth* in 2008. In this particular production, two of my Three Witches had serious attitude problems. I wish I could have translated or transformed their anger into acting, but because their anger manifested itself by their acting bored, it showed in their performances. Their physical demeanor was so casual, it was as if they were not onstage at all.

This is rare. Most actors who appear casual and nonchalant during the rehearsal period rise to the acting occasion on show day, and some even undergo radical transformations. But not these Witches. As a result, our play opened on a strangely un-mysterious note, featuring indifferent, blasé characters.

As director, I blame myself. In retrospect I should have gotten help from someone with dance experience to teach the actors more specific choreography. The actors playing the Witches had mentioned that they were cheerleaders. With better dance choreography and more specific physical directions, they might have had more fun, and dynamic movement might have usurped their bored physical countenance. It is also possible that working with a second adult could have increased their chances of responding positively to directions.

I urge anyone who is putting on a Shakespeare show to seek out qualified helpers in areas such as voice, dance, music, and combat from your own circle of colleagues. There are people nearby who will gladly offer their talents. As an added benefit, it expands your personal and professional network. Sometimes it takes a village to build a Shakespeare play.

In our version of the climactic fight scene between Macbeth and Macduff, a woman played Macbeth and a man depicted Macduff. It is gratifying to have inter-gender fighting in a clash normally enacted by two men. This type of non-traditional casting can shed new light on a scene. It adds a nice modern touch to this classic battle, and the women in both the cast and the audience seemed to appreciate it.

It is challenging to achieve the proper level of emotional intensity in a drama. Some actors are hesitant to embarrass themselves. Sometimes I will stop the scene and have the entire group recite a speech together, starting at a low volume and ending up practically screaming. There is safety in numbers, and when the whole group risks taking the energy to a higher level, the individual is freer to do the same.

The actual killing of Macbeth happens offstage in this version. Macduff re-enters with a slightly deflated volleyball in a sack, which adequately represents a severed head. Of course you have the option of purchasing or manufacturing a severed head prop, but the danger is that this might elicit laughter rather than horror. Still, if somebody in your group feels he or she can make a stab at building a dead head, by all means encourage this. As with pieces of stage business, props and costumes made by cast members contribute to the feeling of ownership of the project, which adds to group unity and pride.

MACBETH: ACT I, SCENE V AND ACT II, SCENES I AND II

I love it when individuals have a naturally dynamic vocal instrument that they discover through acting. This was the case with the actress playing Lady Macbeth in this powerful scene. Lady Macbeth's voice on, "Come you spirits that tend on mortal thoughts, unsex me here," is delivered with a chilling clarity, piercing to the back row of the balcony. By focusing on the impact of Shakespeare's words rather than cluttering the story with props and makeup, the true horror of the story reveals itself through Shakespeare's powerful text and the strong imagination and conviction the actors bring to their characters.

In our 2008 performance, after the line, "The very stones prate of my whereabouts," there should have been an offstage bell ring. That cue did not arrive, so the actress playing Macbeth gave a long pause, and then repeated the line more insistently, to some laughter from the audience. There was a longer pause, as the bell still did not ring. It was clear to me that a bell ringing was not imminent, so I clapped my hands twice from the audience, and Macbeth continued with his next line.

If a cue, whether onstage or offstage, does not appear to be forthcoming, keep going! Macbeth has excellent theatrical momentum in the dagger speech, but it was disrupted and dissipated by delay and laughter due to a botched sound cue. Botched sound cues may be inevitable; therefore one must preemptively prepare a response. If Macbeth had cocked his ear and acted as if he heard a bell, the scene could have continued seamlessly. Not only is "mime hearing" a good acting exercise, but also, in the context of the story itself, if Macbeth can hallucinate a dagger, he can just as easily hallucinate a bell!

A prop, such as a dagger, is a good pointing tool, one that summons Macbeth to heaven (point upward with dagger) or to hell (point downward with dagger). Simple stage directions give you a starting point for physicalizations. They set the wheels in motion, opening up new spontaneous staging ideas in rehearsal that may end up as part of the performance. The pacing is important in this scene. Just as the dagger speech increases in urgency as it continues, so the scene itself become more desperate. Each sound (a knock, a bell, an owl) intensifies Macbeth and Lady Macbeth's terror and brings the scene to its panicked peak.

This play ends with the "Out, out brief candle" soliloquy (from Act V, Scene V), spoken in unison by the group. The actors begin the speech as they walk on stage, and by the time the speech ends, the whole ensemble is center stage with their voices rising. By the time they reach the concluding line, "Signifying nothing!" they are at a full shout, with arms upraised. They then hold hands and go into their triumphant bow. It is quite effective to take a dramatic passage from somewhere else in the script to end the play. It adds a memorable exclamation point to one of Shakespeare's memorable tragedy, one so steeped in mystery and horror that many actors dare not speak its name on the stage, referring to it only as "The Scottish Play."

✳ *MACBETH:* MONOLOGUE NOTES

ACT I, SCENE V: LADY MACBETH MONOLOGUE

In this monologue, Lady Macbeth has just finished reading a letter from Macbeth that details the witches' predictions about his ascent to power. She speaks to herself while also addressing the absent Macbeth using the second person, "thou," "thee," and "thy."

A number of approaches may be used when performing this monologue. Lady Macbeth could simply act as if Macbeth is present, speaking directly to him as if he were in front of her. Alternatively, she could talk to herself alone or to the audience. If speaking to the audience, Lady Macbeth could speak to them as if they were confidantes or as if they were Macbeth. There are numerous choices as to attitude and perspective within every monologue, and experimenting with different options yields a richer understanding of the text and ultimately a stronger performance.

Another way to recite the passage is as if it were a conversation between two people or, more accurately, two sides to Lady Macbeth's thinking. The first sentence in the monologue contains a confident statement: ". . . shalt be what thou art promised." The second sentence contradicts that confidence with a misgiving: "Yet I do fear thy nature." Similarly, in the next sentence, Lady Macbeth again issues a confident claim: "Thou wouldst be great, art not without ambition." In the next breath, she adds, "but without the illness should attend it." Back and forth go Lady Macbeth's thoughts, rising with ambition and falling with unease.

If you are playing Lady Macbeth, you can use voice and body language to illustrate her words, literally rising taller and speaking with bold tones, then catching yourself as you describe the obsta-cles in Macbeth's personality that could keep him from the power she desires for him. "Glamis," "Cawdor," and "what thou art prom-ised" represent three levels of potential achievement for Macbeth, and Lady Macbeth's voice, face, and body language can reflect the ascending tiers of glory that she hopes for Macbeth to achieve.

Under normal circumstances, being "full of the milk of human kindness" is a positive attribute, but Lady Macbeth adds the word "too" in front of the phrase, turning it into a liability. She claims Macbeth lacks "the illness" that should accompany ambition, imply-ing that it is an illness he should have. You can experiment with dif-ferent ways of expressing this dynamic. Try saying the line two ways: once with a vocal tone of "pity but affection," with a softness in the eyes and voice, and next with a vocal tone of sarcasm with a sneer on her face. How do these two approaches depict Lady Macbeth's feeling for her husband?

Lady Macbeth could describe Macbeth's positive attributes—and absence of negative attributes—with warmth and love, or she could color her words with disdain. Perhaps both love and disdain could find their way into her delivery of the words. There are various hues to each monologue, and through a careful mining of the text, you, the studious actor, will arrive at a palette that is uniquely your own.

There is a shift in tone with the line "Hie thee hither." Prior to this line, Lady Macbeth has been describing Macbeth's strengths and weaknesses as they relate to his ability to seize power. This line, however, is a command. Lady Macbeth has a plan, and her verbiage now becomes stronger and more assured. "My spirits," "chastise," "valor," and "tongue" are all words that describe Lady Macbeth's own attributes, ones that she will use to achieve her goals, while "golden round," "fate," "metaphysical aid," and "crowned" describe the outside forces and conditions that will bring the Macbeths to power and glory.

There should be a pause between the first half of the mono-logue—the "questions"—and the second half—the "answer." Lady

Macbeth decides that it is she herself who will direct the next chapter of Macbeth's rise to royalty, and she will orchestrate it with confidence and cunning.

SUGGESTED VIEWING

MACBETH, 1971
Director: Roman Polanski
Starring: Jon Finch, Francesca Annis

MACBETH, 2015
Director: Justin Kurzel
Starring: Michael Fassbender, Marillon Cotillard

✷ THE MERCHANT OF VENICE

CHARACTERS IN THE PLAY

The following is a list of characters that appear in this scene of
The Merchant of Venice.

DUKE OF VENICE
ANTONIO: A merchant of Venice
BASSANIO: A Venetian gentleman, suitor to Portia
SHYLOCK: A Jewish moneylender in Venice
SOLARINO: Companion of Antonio and Bassanio
PORTIA: An heiress of Belmont
NERISSA: Portia's waiting-gentlewoman
BAILIFFS
CHORUS MEMBERS
NARRATOR

SET AND PROP LIST

SET PIECES:
Table
Two stools

PROPS:
Large scroll for Shylock's bond
Bag of coins for Bassanio to offer Shylock
Letter for Nerissa to give to Duke
Knife for Shylock

✳ *THE MERCHANT OF VENICE:* ACT IV, SCENE I

Venice. A court of justice.

Enter NARRATOR *from stage rear, coming downstage center.*

NARRATOR
> In the courtroom, Shylock arrives to claim his pound of flesh from Antonio. *(whispers)* There is a mystery guest.

Exit NARRATOR *stage left.*

Enter DUKE, ANTONIO, *and* BASSANIO *from stage right.*

Drumbeats with a dance rhythm sound from offstage.

Enter CHORUS *from stage right, drumming and dancing.*

DUKE *(stands)*
> *(yells)* Silence!

CHORUS *members stop and scurry to their positions.*

DUKE *sits on center stool and* ANTONIO *sits on stage left stool.*

DUKE
> Antonio, I am sorry for thee: Thou art come
>   to answer
> an inhuman wretch, void and empty
> From any dram of mercy.

ANTONIO
>I am arm'd
>To suffer, with a quietness of spirit,
>The very tyranny and rage of his.

DUKE
>Go one, and call the Jew into the court.

Exit one CHORUS *member stage right to retrieve* SHYLOCK.

Enter SHYLOCK *from stage right, holding a scroll of rolled-up paper: his bond. He sits on stage right stool.*

DUKE *(stands)*
>*(with authority)* Shylock, the world thinks, and I
>   think so too,
>That thou but lead'st this fashion of thy malice
>To the last hour of act; and then 'tis thought
>Thou'lt show thy mercy and remorse more strange
>Than is thy strange apparent cruelty;
>We all expect a gentle answer, Jew.

SHYLOCK *(stands)*
>By our holy Sabbath have I sworn
>To have the due and forfeit of my bond:
>I give no reason, nor I will not,
>More than a lodged hate and a certain loathing
>I bear Antonio.
>Are you answer'd?

CHORUS *answers, "No!" and general pandemonium follows.*

BASSANIO *(angrily steps toward* SHYLOCK*)*
>This is no answer, thou unfeeling man.
>For thy three thousand ducats here is six.
>   *(hands* SHYLOCK *bag of money)*

SHYLOCK *looks into the bag, swallows hard, and drops it at* BAS-
SANIO'S *feet.* CHORUS *utters, "Ooh!" in response.*

SHYLOCK
> If every ducat in six thousand ducats
> Were in six parts and every part a ducat,
> *(very distinctly)* I would not draw them; I would
>   have my bond.

DUKE *(still standing)*
> How shalt thou hope for mercy, rendering none?

SHYLOCK *(walks downstage right, away from the others)*
> What judgment shall I dread, doing no wrong?
> You have among you many a purchased slave,
> Which, like your asses and your dogs and mules,
> You use in abject and in slavish parts,
> Because you bought them.
> The pound of flesh, which I demand of him,
> Is dearly bought; 'tis mine and (distinctly) I will
>   have it.

SHYLOCK *takes out knife and* CHORUS *cries, "No!"*

Enter SOLARINO *from stage right.*

SOLARINO
> My lord, here stays without
> A messenger with letters from the doctor,
> New come from Padua.

DUKE
> Bring us the letter; call the messenger.

Exit SOLARINO *stage right to retrieve* NERISSA.

Enter NERISSA *from stage right, dressed as a lawyer's clerk. She bows to* DUKE.

DUKE

Came you from Padua, from Bellario?

NERISSA

From both, my lord. Bellario greets your grace.

NERISSA *presents a letter to* DUKE. DUKE *reads the letter to himself.*

DUKE

This letter from Bellario doth commend
A young and learned doctor to our court.
Where is he?

NERISSA

He attendeth here hard by. *(points stage right)*

Enter PORTIA *from stage right, as* BALTHAZAR, *a doctor of laws.*

DUKE

And here, I take it, is the doctor come.
Give me your hand. Come you from old Bellario?

PORTIA *comes center, starts to curtsy but catches herself, and then bows to* DUKE. *Meanwhile,* SHYLOCK *walks upstage to sit on stage right stool.*

PORTIA

I did, my lord.
I am informed thoroughly of the cause.
Which is the merchant here, and which the Jew?

SHYLOCK *(stands)*
> Shylock is my name.

PORTIA
> *(to* **ANTONIO***)* You stand within his danger,
>> do you not?

ANTONIO *(stands)*
> Ay, so he says.

PORTIA
> Do you confess the bond?

ANTONIO
> I do.

PORTIA
> Then must the Jew be merciful.

SHYLOCK *(animated and agitated)*
> On what compulsion must I? Tell me that.

PORTIA *gestures for* **SHYLOCK** *to sit;* **SHYLOCK** *sits.*

PORTIA
> The quality of mercy is not strained.
> It droppeth as the gentle rain from heaven
> Upon the place beneath. It is twice blest:
> It blesseth him that gives and him that takes.
> 'Tis mightiest in the mightiest; it becomes
> The thronèd monarch better than his crown.
> His scepter shows the force of temporal power,
> The attribute to awe and majesty
> Wherein doth sit the dread and fear of kings;
> But mercy is above this sceptered sway.
> It is enthronèd in the hearts of kings;

It is an attribute to God Himself;
And earthly power doth then show likest God's
When mercy seasons justice. Therefore, Jew,
Though justice be thy plea, consider this:
That in the course of justice none of us
Should see salvation. We do pray for mercy,
And that same prayer doth teach us all to render
The deeds of mercy. I have spoke thus much
To mitigate the justice of thy plea,
Which, if thou follow, this strict court of Venice
Must needs give sentence 'gainst the merchant there.

SHYLOCK *(stands, agitated)*

My deeds upon my head! I crave the law,
The penalty and forfeit of my bond.

PORTIA

I pray you, let me look upon the bond. *(takes bond
from* **SHYLOCK***)*
Why, this bond is forfeit;
And lawfully by this the Jew may claim
A pound of flesh, to be by him cut off
Nearest the merchant's heart. Be merciful:

PORTIA *kneels at* **SHYLOCK'S** *stool and softly pleads with him.*

Take twice thy money; bid me tear the bond.

SHYLOCK *(stares at* **PORTIA***)*

(firmly) There is no power in the tongue of man
To alter me: I stay here on my bond.

PORTIA

Why then, thus it is: *(hands the bond back to*
SHYLOCK *and turns to* **ANTONIO***)*
You must prepare your bosom for his knife.

DUKE *motions two* BAILIFFS *to stand over* ANTONIO. *They do so, with* BASSANIO *acting threatening toward* BAILIFFS *by standing between them and* ANTONIO. DUKE *waves* BASSANIO *back.*

SHYLOCK

We trifle time: I pray thee, pursue sentence.

Dramatic drumbeat sounds from offstage.

SHYLOCK *sharpens his knife and approaches* ANTONIO. CHORUS *murmurs and grows noisy. As* SHYLOCK *draws close, he brings knife up over his head.* CHORUS *gasps.*

PORTIA

Tarry a little; (PORTIA *moves between* SHYLOCK *and* ANTONIO) there is something else.
This bond doth give thee here no jot of blood;
The words expressly are "a pound of flesh."
Take then thy bond, take thou thy pound of flesh;
But, in the cutting it, if thou dost shed
One drop of Christian blood, thy lands and goods
Are, by the laws of Venice, confiscate
Unto the state of Venice.

SHYLOCK

Is that the law?

PORTIA

Thyself shalt see the act:

PORTIA *shows* SHYLOCK *the passage in the bond. He examines it carefully.*

For, as thou urgest justice, be assured
Thou shalt have justice, more than thou desirest.
Therefore prepare thee to cut off the flesh.

> Shed thou no blood, nor cut thou less nor more
> But just a pound of flesh: If the scale do turn
> But in the estimation of a hair,
> Thou diest and all thy goods are confiscate.

SHYLOCK *(incredulous and stunned)*
> *(sits)* Give me my principal, and let me go.

SHYLOCK *returns bond to* **PORTIA** *and holds his hand out for the money.*

PORTIA
> Thou shalt have nothing but the forfeiture,
> To be so taken at thy peril, Jew.

ALL *whisper, "Jew."*

SHYLOCK
> I'll stay no longer. *(stands)*

PORTIA
> Tarry, Jew:

PORTIA *motions for* **SHYLOCK** *to sit down; he refuses.*

ALL *repeat, "Jew," louder and point.* **SHYLOCK** *sits.*

> The law hath yet another hold on you.
> It is enacted in the laws of Venice,
> If it be proved against an alien

CHORUS *says, "Jew!" more loudly and points.*

> That by direct or indirect attempts
> He seek the life of any citizen,
> The party 'gainst the which he doth contrive
> Shall seize one half his goods; the other half

Comes to the privy coffer of the state;
And the offender's life lies in the mercy
Of the duke only.
Down therefore and beg mercy of the duke.
(points for SHYLOCK *to kneel)*

SHYLOCK *refuses.* ALL *repeat,* "*Down.*" SHYLOCK *kneels.*

DUKE

That thou shalt see the difference of our spirits,
I pardon thee thy life before thou ask it:
For half thy wealth, it is Antonio's;
The other half comes to the general state.

SHYLOCK

Nay, take my life and all; pardon not that:
You take my life
When you do take the means whereby I live.

PORTIA

What mercy can you render him, Antonio?

ANTONIO

So please my lord the Duke and all the court
To quit the fine for one half of his goods,
I am content; More, that, for this favor,
He presently become a Christian.

PORTIA

Art thou contented, Jew? What dost thou say?

SHYLOCK *(defeated)*

I am content.
I pray you, give me leave to go from hence;
I am not well.

DUKE
Get thee gone.

Exit SHYLOCK *stage right.*

PORTIA *(to* BASSANIO, *mysteriously, with a hint of a smile)*
I pray you, know me when we meet again:
I wish you well, and so I take my leave.

BASSANIO *appears puzzled by* PORTIA'S *words.*

Military drumbeat sounds from offstage.

ALL *exit stage left, somberly.*

✳ *THE MERCHANT OF VENICE:* PERFORMANCE NOTES

I directed this production of *The Merchant of Venice* in 2013 with a group of high school seniors. Although the play is technically a "comedy," it is also one of Shakespeare's cruelest, depicting the harsh treatment of Shylock as well as an attitude of prejudice toward the Jewish people.

Discuss with your castmates what experiences they may have had with prejudice. Look at the individual characters to explore what good and bad qualities they exhibit personally. Through examining our own experiences with intolerance, and by looking at discrimination through the eyes of Shakespeare's characters, we can better portray the complex individuals and relationships in this riveting drama.

The subject is one that is painful and touchy to examine, but in the context of drama and history, the issue of prejudice can be explored in a way that is equally healthy and revelatory. Both Shylock and Antonio have sympathetic and unkind qualities. By showing more than one side to their characters, actors paint a nuanced dramatic picture that allows us to see what motivates people to behave in objectionable ways. When we experience Shylock as a living, breathing human with noble qualities as well as tragic flaws, Shakespeare's words and stories have greater emotional depth and a deeper personal impact.

I used a Chorus extensively in this production: in the "courting" scenes as an entourage to the Princes and Bassanio, as well as in the courtroom scene as a jury or gallery. There are several advantages to choral work. First, it strengthens the group dynamic. Actors who would otherwise have minor roles are onstage for longer, allowing for a greater level of participation. This contributes greatly to the overall feel of the performance as an ensemble production.

Simultaneous actions by characters with speaking parts and the Chorus impart tightness to the visual theatrics. When one character drew the "curtains," he made a clean gesture with both hands from the center of his body, which was echoed by the Chorus. Likewise, when he raised his hands up, the Chorus makes the same gesture simultaneously. This use of the Chorus keeps more students engaged in the performance and rehearsals, significantly enhances the ensemble feel of the play, and provides a nod back to classical theater by using a technique made popular by the Greek chorus.

In addition, the Chorus reinforces the mood: When the action is funny, the Chorus makes it funnier! In one scene, all six Chorus members bump into Bassanio and each other, a comic moment that would have been far less effective with only one collision. Likewise, when the mood is harsher, the Chorus makes it downright brutal. When all the actors onstage shout, "Jew!" and point to Shylock, the impact is greater than if only one character had done so. The Chorus provides visual and sound effects, verbal commentary, and emotional reactions to the action on the stage, which not only helps clarify the story but also adds to its power.

We had to work hard to achieve the unity of word and gesture that we were seeking. When one Chorus member is off, the whole group suffers. This is why we rehearse until we get it right. I consider this ensemble work to be one of the greater rewards of putting on a play. It is gratifying to watch performers experience the satisfaction of a successful group effort.

I am always amazed at how a simple gesture can change a theatrical moment for the better. The narrator in one scene spoke the line, "Next up is the Prince of Arragon. Will he fare any better? Place your bets." This is the kind of line that could evoke a laugh but could just as easily fall flat. The actor playing the narrator chose to remove his hat from his head when saying, "Place your bets," holding the hat out toward the audience as if to collect money. He paused a second before doing so, which added an element of surprise and got a laugh. At every moment in a play, you can make small choices, either through gesture, inflection, timing, or facial expression, to change the tone and even the meaning of a scene.

THE MERCHANT OF VENICE: ACT IV, SCENE I

The courtroom scene opens with a dance drumbeat (repeating a bit from previous scenes) to usher in the Chorus, who dances in, only to have the Duke stand up and yell, "Silence!" prompting them to stop dead in their tracks, unsmiling. This sets the tone for a scene that is definitively non-comedic. Antonio sits on the stool with his arms tied. When Shylock defends his insistence on a pound of Antonio's flesh, and asks, "Are you answered?" the Chorus, as one, sternly replies, "No!"

In Portia's speech explaining to Shylock his punishment if he sheds a drop of Christian blood, every time Portia says the word "Jew," the Chorus repeats it, first in a whisper, then louder, pointing fingers, and finally yelling the word at Shylock. The effect of this group speech and gesture is chilling. The Chorus, which before was dancing and silly, is now vindictive and cruel.

Just as comedy is funnier under a backdrop of sadness, so is tragedy more poignant when it has been preceded by laughter. *The Merchant of Venice* balances these comic and cruel elements masterfully as the Chorus points to Shylock and brings him to his knees as they yell, "Down!" In drama, a character will change as events unfold, and the actor playing Shylock did an excellent job of depicting Shylock's transformation from a proud and haughty merchant to a beaten, pleading man.

Shakespeare's *The Merchant of Venice* is a powerful play with themes of bigotry and intolerance that apply to any era. By experiencing this timeless story together, our ensemble and the audience gained insight into what motivates human cruelty, with enough levity provided to make us laugh.

Live theater is magical. It is the most dynamic form of entertainment available to us. *The Merchant of Venice* is a powerful drama, and we are fortunate to be able to keep giving the story life, particularly with performers who can give the play the vitality it deserves.

✳ *THE MERCHANT OF VENICE:* MONOLOGUE NOTES

ACT IV, SCENE I: PORTIA (AS BALTHAZAR) MONOLOGUE

Portia is twice disguised in this scene: She is pretending to be a man, and she is also masquerading as a lawyer ("Balthazar"). Shylock, who has the law on his side in requesting a pound of Antonio's flesh as punishment for failure to repay a loan on time, has had the upper hand in the proceedings thus far. Despite the falseness of her charade, Portia's words must ring true with regard to their message: her heartfelt hope that Shylock show compassion.

To what extent must Portia continue to attempt to conceal her true identity in this passage? Should she move and speak in a "manly" and "lawyerly" fashion? Clearly it is in her interest to maintain this façade, but to do too much of it would detract from the genuine quality of the speech. As Balthazar, hold yourself with excellent posture and speak your words with authority, but do not force your voice into a significantly lower range just to give the impression of masculinity. You must speak naturally for the monologue to come across as heartfelt.

The speech is written largely in iambic pentameter, but there are several lines that contain an extra syllable. When this occurs, I look at the text to see if there appears to be a reason for this. If we look at the iambic pentameter rhythm as a heartbeat, an extra line might indicate that the speaker's heart has skipped a beat due to an emotional or physical response to something in the text. Even when this interpretation does not seem to apply, an extra beat in what is normally a line of iambic pentameter should be recognized and possibly acted upon.

The first instance of an additional syllable occurs in the second line: "It droppeth as the gentle rain from heaven." The word "heaven" could be contracted ("heav'n") to sound like one syllable, but I suggest giving the word its poetic power and pausing slightly before saying it. This will give "heaven" more prominence and convey its full impact to the listener. Though the word is at the end of the line, you must continue through to the next line until you reach the end of the sentence. In general, if the end of a line is in the middle of a sentence, do not stop! Aside from moments in which you are consciously choosing to pause, let the punctuation, and not the word's position in the line, determine your stopping points.

After Portia says, "It is twice blest," she describes several examples of the "double blessing" of mercy. On the line "It blesseth him that gives and him that takes," you might add a gesture with each hand palm up and out to the side as if balancing your hands like the scales of justice.

In the next few lines, Portia outlines the difference between the temporal power of the king's scepter (i.e., a power that is wordly and void of any sacred qualities) and the more spiritual force of mercy, which is "enthroned in the hearts of kings." To give the speech its full impact, it will be helpful to decide which words to emphasize here. In the 2004 film version of *The Merchant of Venice*, starring Al Pacino and Joseph Fiennes, the actress playing Portia (Lynn Collins) chose to place emphasis on the following words: "But mercy is **above** this sceptered sway./It is enthroned in the **hearts** of kings/It is an attribute to **God** Himself."

Why did she choose those three words? First, examine the rhythmic structure. The emphasized words are in the center of each line. On the first line, she accents the third beat (out of five), and on the next two lines she highlights the fourth beat.

Notice also that the words she focuses on are all spiritual in connotation. "Above" can allude to heaven. The "heart" is presumed to be the seat of love, and "God Himself" is perhaps the highest of all powers. Try accenting the word "mercy," too, and then speak the line again without this emphasis. Is there a difference to your ear? To fully flesh out these speeches, it helps to say them out loud to yourself in various ways: stressing different words, experimenting with dynamics of volume, and trying different physical gestures in front of a mirror or video camera.

Monologue work is comprehensive: It engages our intellectual, emotional, spiritual, and physical qualities and asks the actor to unify those characteristics into a piece of theatre that resonates with the audience on several levels. If Portia simply looks up a little when she says the words "above" and "God," she might create a subtle visual cue for viewers, pointing out the "high" nature of mercy. Likewise when she refers to "earthly power" in the next line, she can gesture downward.

These are simple physical movements, but when done sparingly and at the appropriate moment, they can add visual texture to the speech and enhance the words' meaning. I envision Portia's hands to be like the classic "scales of justice" when she says, "When mercy seasons justice." I have referenced the physical gesture of "scales of justice" earlier in these notes, and here again is another possibility for using that same motion. You can place your right hand to the side on the word "mercy," and your left hand to the other side on "justice," then bring the hands up and down as if to balance the two.

You will need to decide when to use this physical action in the piece since you want to avoid repeating the same movements too many times. We want to keep it subtle and tasteful. We don't want to hammer our point home; we want the audience to fill in some of the images with their own imaginations. Thus, physical gestures of this sort are more effective if used economically, but they do have their dramatic power. Experiment in front of a mirror and decide where—if at all—you want to use the gesture.

The monologue changes mood with the following words: "Therefore, Jew..." Until this point, Portia has not referred to Shylock by name or race. She has been talking to him as a fellow human. The word "Jew" here is jarring because it brings us back to Shylock's Jewishness. In describing mercy, Portia never refers to any ethnicity. Try playing the word "Jew" as a pivotal word that brings Portia back into the character of Balthazar, which forces her to recommit to the charade that she is a male lawyer. In other words, the word "Jew" brings Portia back to the legal business at hand. Portia might return to a more masculine and lawyerly demeanor here, as if her talk of mercy was more Portia talking than Balthazar. Square your shoulders. Lower the pitch of your voice a little. Take a couple of authoritative steps toward Shylock.

The closing lines might be more presentational, delivered for the benefit of the courtroom and the audience, whereas Portia's talk of mercy was directed more at Shylock. Look out to the audience as if they are members of the courtroom. Portia continues to exhort Shylock to show mercy on Bassanio, but her tone is more official. Notice how she repeats the word "justice" three times in the final three sentences. Give a stern quality to the words "strict" and "sentence" by emphasizing the "s" and "t" sounds and bouncing the clipped consonants off your tongue.

Portia is a female heiress, but in this scene she plays a male lawyer. Determine at which points the "real" Portia emerges in the monologue and where she is more likely to be acting as Balthazar. This will showcase your acting ability and clarify the dynamics of the speech to the audience. Portia's gentler qualities could dominate the first part of the monologue. Consider making "Therefore, Jew" a turning point and have "Balthazar" and his legal acumen finish the speech from there.

Again, it is important to know how the scene—and the play—ends. Portia/Balthazar does indeed impose a very harsh sentence on Shylock. After this monologue, Portia advises the court that if Shylock spills a "jot of blood" or takes any more or less than an exact pound of flesh, he will die and all his goods will be confiscated. Perhaps her own mercy has its limits when Shylock shows no compassion himself.

This is one of Shakespeare's more famous speeches because it addresses the "quality of mercy" in a poetic and timeless fashion, using elegant phrases and beautifully descriptive language and imagery. Enjoy portraying Portia as Balthazar, a character who displays both the gentleness of mercy and the cruelty of justice.

SUGGESTED VIEWING

THE MERCHANT OF VENICE, 1973
Director: John Sichel
Starring: Laurence Olivier, Joan Plowright

THE MERCHANT OF VENICE, 2004
Director: Michael Radford
Starring: Al Pacino, Joseph Fiennes, Lynn Collins

✳ THE MERRY WIVES OF WINDSOR

CHARACTERS IN THE PLAY

The following is a list of characters that appear in this scene of
The Merry Wives of Windsor.

SIR JOHN FALSTAFF: A knight
MISTRESS ALICE FORD
MISTRESS MARGARET PAGE
PISTOL: Follower of Falstaff
DR. CAIUS: A French physician
MISTRESS QUICKLY: Servant to Dr. Caius
MASTER FRANCIS FORD ⎤
MASTER GEORGE PAGE ⎦ Gentlemen of Windsor
SIR HUGH EVANS: A Welsh parson
SERVANTS
NARRATOR

SET AND PROP LIST

SET PIECES:
Trees

PROPS:

Leaves
Buck's head or deer antlers for Falstaff
Drums
Masks
Wand for Mistress Quickly

✳ *THE MERRY WIVES OF WINDSOR:*
ACT V, SCENE V

Windsor Forest.

Enter **NARRATOR** *from stage rear, coming downstage left.*

NARRATOR
> The Merry Wives have convinced Falstaff to dress up as Herne the Hunter, a folk hero who has antlers on his head. They promise to meet him in the woods, where many of our players have disguised themselves as fairies to have their comeuppance on the fat fool Falstaff.

Exit **NARRATOR** *stage left.*

SOUND OPERATOR *plays* Sound Cue #1 ("Forest sounds").

Enter **SIR JOHN FALSTAFF** *wearing a buck's head.*

FALSTAFF
> The Windsor bell hath struck twelve. The minute draws on. Now, the hot-blooded gods assist me! Remember, Jove, thou wast a bull for thy Europa; love set on thy horns. O powerful love, that in some respects makes a beast a man, in some other a man a beast! You were also, Jupiter, a swan for the love of Leda. O omnipotent love, how near the god drew to the complexion of a goose! A fault done first in the form of a beast; O Jove, a beastly fault! And then another fault

in the semblance of a fowl; think on 't, Jove, a foul
fault. When gods have hot backs, what shall poor men
do? For me, I am here a Windsor stag, and the fattest,
I think, i' th' forest. Send me a cool rut-time, Jove, or
who can blame me to piss
my tallow?

Enter MISTRESS PAGE *and* MISTRESS FORD.

Who comes here? My doe?

MISTRESS FORD

Sir John! Art thou there, my deer? My male deer?
(caresses his antlers)

FALSTAFF

My doe with the black scut! Let the sky rain
potatoes; let there come a tempest of provocation,
I will shelter me here.

MISTRESS FORD

Mistress Page is come with me, sweetheart.

MISTRESS PAGE *and* MISTRESS FORD *place themselves on either
side of* FALSTAFF, *and he puts his arms around them. It is his
great moment of pleasure!*

FALSTAFF

Divide me like a bribe buck, each a haunch: Am I a
woodman, ha? Speak I like Herne the hunter? As I
am a true spirit, welcome!

SOUND OPERATOR *plays* Sound Cue #2 ("Fairy music
and drumbeats").

MISTRESS PAGE

Alas, what noise?

MISTRESS FORD

Heaven forgive our sins.

FALSTAFF

What should this be?

MISTRESS FORD AND MISTRESS PAGE

Away, away!

Exit MISTRESS FORD *and* MISTRESS PAGE *stage left, hurriedly.*

Enter MISTRESS QUICKLY, FORD *(with drum),* PAGE, DR. CAIUS, SIR HUGH EVANS *(disguised with mask), and* PISTOL *(as Hobgoblin) from stage right. Others, as* FAIRIES, *also enter from stage right, following* MISTRESS QUICKLY, *who dances across the stage with her wand and directs them to form a semicircle behind* FALSTAFF.

MISTRESS QUICKLY

Fairies, black, grey, green, and white,
You moonshine revellers and shades of night,
You orphan heirs of fixed destiny,
Attend your office and your quality.

FALSTAFF

They are fairies; he that speaks to them shall die:
I'll wink and couch: No man their works must eye.
(lies face-down on the ground)

MISTRESS QUICKLY

About, about;
Search Windsor Castle, elves, within and out:
And "Honi soit qui mal y pense" write

In emerald tufts, flowers purple, blue, and white;
Our dance of custom round about the oak
Of Herne the hunter, let us not forget.

SIR HUGH EVANS

Pray you, lock hand in hand; (ALL *join hands*
and start to circle around FALSTAFF) yourselves
in order set
And twenty glow-worms shall our lanterns be,
To guide our measure round about the tree.
(*circle divides to form a semicircle behind*
FALSTAFF *again;* SIR HUGH *sniffs at the air*)
But, stay; I smell a man of middle-earth.

FALSTAFF

Heavens defend me from that Welsh fairy, lest he
transform me to a piece of cheese!

PISTOL (*lunging at him*)
Vile worm, thou wast o'erlook'd even in thy birth.

MISTRESS QUICKLY

With trial-fire touch me his finger-end:
If he be chaste, the flame will back descend
And turn him to no pain; but if he start,
It is the flesh of a corrupted heart.

PISTOL

A trial, come.

ALL *lunge at* FALSTAFF, *fiercely yelling, "Aaaaaah!"*

FALSTAFF

Oh, Oh, Oh!

MISTRESS QUICKLY
> Corrupt, corrupt, and tainted in desire!
> About him, fairies; sing a scornful rhyme;
> And, as you trip, still pinch him to your time.

In the song that follows, characters sing individual lines.
On bold words, ALL *sing* AND *point at* FALSTAFF.

MISTRESS QUICKLY
> Fie on sinful fantasy!
> Fie on lust and luxury!

FORD
> Lust is but a bloody fire,
> Kindled with unchaste desire.

SERVANT
> Fed in heart, whose flames aspire
> As thoughts do blow them, higher and higher.

DR. CAIUS
> Pinch him, fairies, mutually; *(they pinch him)*
> Pinch him for his villany.

SIR HUGH EVANS
> Pinch him, and burn him, and turn him about,
> Till candles and starlight and moonshine be out!

ALL *lunge at* FALSTAFF, *yelling "Aaaaaah!" until he is shivering,*
cringing, and near tears.

MISTRESS PAGE *(taking pity and compassion on him)*
> I pray you, come, hold up the jest no higher.
> *(takes off her mask)*
> Now, good Sir John, how like you Windsor wives?

FORD *(takes off his mask)*
> Now, sir, who's a cuckold now? Falstaff's a knave, a
> cuckoldly knave; here are his horns, he hath enjoyed
> nothing of Ford's but his buck-basket!

MISTRESS FORD *(takes off her mask)*
> Sir John, we have had ill luck; we could never meet.
> I will never take you for my love again; but I will
> always count you my deer.

FALSTAFF
> I do begin to perceive that I am made an ass.

FORD
> Ay, and an ox too: Both the proofs are extant.

FALSTAFF
> And these are not fairies? *(FAIRIES remove their
> masks and laugh)* Well, I am your theme: You have
> the start of me; I am dejected; use me as you will.
> *(bows his head in shame and humility)*

PAGE *(helps him up)*
> Yet be cheerful, knight: Thou shalt eat a posset
> tonight at my house; where I will desire thee to
> laugh at my wife, that now laughs at thee.

FORD
> Stand not amazed; here is no remedy:
> In love the heavens themselves do guide the state;
> Money buys lands, and wives are sold by fate.

FALSTAFF
> I am glad, though you have ta'en a special stand to
> strike at me, that your arrow hath glanced.

MISTRESS PAGE
Well, I will muse no further.
Heaven give you many, many merry days!
Good husband, let us every one go home,
And laugh this sport o'er by a country fire;
Sir John and all. *(laughs as others join in)*

ALL *hold hands and take a bow. Exeunt.*

✳ THE MERRY WIVES OF WINDSOR: PERFORMANCE NOTES

Shakespeare's *The Merry Wives of Windsor* is dear to my heart, as I performed in the Folger Theatre's 1986 production of the play. The staging featured a circus motif, and I played Jack Rugby, servant to Dr. Caius, a small role that was transformed into a juggler's part to take advantage of my specific skills. Mistress Quickly was played in drag, Master and Mistress Ford in whiteface, and Master and Mistress Page as commedia dell'arte characters. Sir John Falstaff was a bumbling clown with big shoes and a red nose.

Although the 1998 production of *The Merry Wives of Windsor* that I directed was not circus-themed, I tried to keep that same spirit of mayhem in the performance. I was fortunate to have a ninth grader as Falstaff who embodied that character's infectious charm and self adoring buffoonery. Falstaff's entourage, Pistol, Nym, and young Robin, are cartoonish in word and deed. With the addition of Sir Hugh Evans and Dr. Caius, who both make a joke out of the English language, the play provides hearty laughs in a madcap comedy.

As the narrator introduced the first scene, I had the players cross the stage in character. This is effective for a number of reasons: It sets a fun tone while introducing the main characters to the audience, and it gives you an opportunity to get into character. You must search for personality traits or mannerisms you can physicalize. Audiences need to get their bearings during Shakespeare plays. The language is daunting for them, especially initially. By clarifying character traits and relationships early, sometimes through physical means, we can help the audience relax into the play, allowing the story and language to work their magic.

The actor playing Bardolph in our production knew how to juggle. If you have a special skill, try to find a place for it in the play. Bardolph is a drunk, so giving him juggling skills provided a delicious irony. On one of his lines, "It is a life that I have desired: I will thrive!" he stood on a chair, which added a nice dimension to the staging. In performance, this moment was too short. The actor playing Bardolph stopped juggling and descended from the chair just as the audience applause was rising. Excessive haste is common among novice actors, so try not to step on audience applause or laughter. Because most rehearsals are conducted with no onlookers present, it is helpful to have a small audience at some of the final rehearsals, giving you a chance to adjust for laughter and other possible crowd responses.

Look for breathing points in Shakespearean passages, as well as beats, or moments in a line that indicate a shift in the character's thought, emotion, or action. Mark pauses and beats in your script, which will go a long way toward maintaining rhythm and pacing. It will also help prevent you from running out of breath in the middle of a line!

There are numerous language gags in *The Merry Wives of Windsor*. Pistol speaks in pirate-like bursts of colorful language ("Let vultures gripe thy guts!") and Nym uses the word "humor" in almost every sentence. The best example of linguistic funny business in this production came from Dr. Caius. In addition to a thick French accent, our actress chose to place the accent on the wrong syllable when she spoke. Thus, a phrase like "*ho*-nest *wo*-man" became "ho-nest*wo*-*man*." This incongruity added another layer of absurdity to an already hilarious character. Even in a farcical romp, Shakespeare's language and characters are so rich that you can paint a colorful theatrical picture for the audience. Performing comedy can be very rewarding, especially in the hands of actors discovering Shakespeare for the first time.

THE MERRY WIVES OF WINDSOR: ACT V, SCENE V

The scene changes in this play take place at breakneck speed, another component of presenting an entertaining and fast-paced show. I tell the actors that the stage should never be bare. As in a relay race, when one player exits, the other should be entering, so the action never breaks. I try to instill in my cast the importance of giving focus on stage. They must support their fellow actors by committing to the relationships and the drama. Only by actors' dedication to stage moments can the audience fully enter the world of the play.

Falstaff enters the final scene to New Age music, wearing a pair of deer antlers. He leads with his nose, prances and stamps, clearly reveling in his role. As a member of the gang of fairies, Master Ford plays a large tom-tom drum. Following the accented syllables of the fairies' song, he leans in close to a cowering Falstaff and points at him accusingly with the drumstick. The assembled cast encircles Falstaff and menaces him with key words: "fie," "lust," "kindled," and "pinch." On the word "pinch," the group members lunge in and pinch poor Falstaff, who ends up lying on his back, writhing and spread-eagled on the stage. It is a dramatic stage picture, painted by the entire ensemble in unison.

This production was enacted by a group of ninth graders in a D.C. public school. Ninth graders are at the bottom of the high school totem pole, but after this group of freshmen used Shakespeare's beautiful language and colorful characters to perform his merry tale to a laughing, applauding audience, they were on top of the world. May this be your story, too.

✳ *THE MERRY WIVES OF WINDSOR:* MONOLOGUE NOTES

ACT V, SCENE V: FALSTAFF MONOLOGUE

In this final scene of *The Merry Wives of Windsor,* Falstaff is disguised as a buck. The actor playing Falstaff is then playing the part of somebody playing a part. Falstaff can snort and stomp his feet as if he is a stag excitedly awaiting a doe.

Falstaff has come to the woods hoping to achieve his reward, the prize he has been seeking throughout the play: the love of both Mrs. Ford and Mrs. Page. A few lines later, when the two women arrive, Falstaff exclaims, "Divide me like a bribed buck, each a haunch." His joy is short-lived as he is quickly tormented and brought down to earth by the vengeful villagers. During this monologue, however, Falstaff is quivering with anticipation.

In his first line, Falstaff states, "The Windsor bell hath struck twelve." If the line were part of an actual staged scene, church bells would likely ring audibly. If the monologue is performed solo, the actor can cock his head and pause as if hearing bells.

Falstaff is not just talking to himself; he also makes several direct addresses to Jove, the King of the Gods, sometimes known as Jupiter. Perhaps Falstaff can look up when addressing Jove and look down when referring to himself. Throughout the monologue, Falstaff's words paint contrasting images, ranging from the sublime ("gods," "Jove," "Europa," "omnipotent," and "love") to the earthly ("hot-blooded," "beast," "hot backs," "rut-time," and "piss my tallow").

The sublime words have a different color and texture than the earthly words, and the actor can use contrasting physical gestures and facial expressions to accompany them. Perhaps in addition to looking upward when addressing Jove, Falstaff could raise his arms plaintively as if requesting a boon. By contrast, when referring to "beast," a word he says four times during this speech, Falstaff could sniff the air or jut his jaw forward. Playing the contrasts described in the text—God/man, man/beast—gives Falstaff vocal and physical fodder to provide the scene with drama and dynamics.

Interestingly, Falstaff's words ultimately depict the gods themselves as having human shortcomings. The tone shifts when Falstaff refers to Jupiter taking on the shape of a swan, referring to it as a "foul fault." Could Falstaff pause here, become amused by his own joke, and then laugh? Look for moments in the speech where a pause can allow the audience to laugh or the character to react to his own words. Falstaff justifies his own human fallibilities when he describes the gods themselves as equally flawed.

Try playing the scene in different ways, first brazenly and with bravado and then more contritely, almost apologetically. See what these two approaches offer you as a performer. Falstaff could begin the speech quietly and then raise the volume on "O powerful love." The volume and energy could remain high through "What shall poor men do?" He could turn the volume back down on "For me, I am here a Windsor stag, and the fattest, I think, i' th' forest." Falstaff could play this line ruefully and with a tinge of self-consciousness and vulnerability or simply with a jolly laugh at his own portliness and the funny image of a fat deer. Perhaps the most nuanced performance is not one-dimensional. Falstaff could be simultaneously ashamed of his weight and light-hearted about the fact. The choice is yours: Experiment!

Where are the pauses and breathing points in this speech? When Falstaff pauses, is he looking and listening for signs of his mates? The actor should stay in the imaginary setting. Likewise, if the player is not wearing a costume for the monologue, he should continue to act as if he has on a mask, antlers, and perhaps a fur cape.

Make sure to understand what the phrases mean ("hot backs," "rut-time," "piss my tallow"), who the gods are ("Jove," "Europa," "Jupiter," "Leda"), and the mythological stories Falstaff refers to. When you encounter a proper noun or historical reference, take the time to look it up. You will find great rewards, as a small amount of research can round out your understanding of the character, story, and themes in the text.

Falstaff is a fascinating character, one who is at once bumbling and erudite. He possesses many charms, but he also has a pathetic side. He is not one-dimensional. In many ways, Falstaff has godly qualities—or so he would like to believe. Here he is in the forest, teetering between man and beast, but ultimately he is human and must be brought down to earth with the rest of us. Enjoy playing this unique creation of Shakespeare's imagination. Personalize the performance, and infuse the character with your own singular gifts.

SUGGESTED VIEWING

THE MERRY WIVES OF WINDSOR, 1972
Director: David Hugh Jones
Starring: Richard Griffiths, Judy Davis

THE MERRY WIVES OF WINDSOR, 2011
Director: Christopher Luscombe
Starring: Christopher Benjamin, Sarah Woodward

✴ A MIDSUMMER NIGHT'S DREAM

CHARACTERS IN THE PLAY

The following is a list of characters that appear in this scene of
A Midsummer Night's Dream.

HERMIA
LYSANDER | Four lovers
HELENA
DEMETRIUS
NICK BOTTOM THE WEAVER
TITANIA: Queen of the Fairies
OBERON: King of the Fairies
ROBIN GOODFELLOW (PUCK): A hobgoblin in Oberon's service
PEAS-BLOSSOM
COBWEB | Fairies attending upon Titania
MUSTARD-SEED
THESEUS: Duke of Athens, father to Hermia
HIPPOLYTA: Queen of the Amazons
EGEUS: Father to Hermia
LORDS AND ATTENDANTS ON THESEUS AND HIPPOLYTA
FAIRIES IN THE TRAINS OF TITANIA AND OBERON
NARRATOR

SET AND PROP LIST

SET PIECES:
Trees
Two benches

PROPS:
Ass head for Bottom
Flower for Titania
Scarves and wands for Fairies
Nectar for Oberon
Tambourine for Attendant

✳ *A MIDSUMMER NIGHT'S DREAM:*
ACT IV, SCENE I

The wood.

Enter **NARRATOR** *from rear, coming downstage center.*

NARRATOR
> Through magical fairy mischief, Bottom the Weaver
> has been transformed into an ass, and Titania,
> Queen of the Fairies, has fallen in love with him.
> We are still in the woods . . .

LYSANDER, DEMETRIUS, HELENA, *and* **HERMIA** *are lying asleep.*
Enter **TITANIA** *and* **BOTTOM; PEAS-BLOSSOM, COBWEB, MOTH,**
MUSTARD-SEED, *and other* **FAIRIES** *attending;* **OBERON** *behind*
unseen. All enter from stage rear.

TITANIA *(to* **BOTTOM***)*
> Come, sit thee down upon this flowery bed,
> While I thy amiable cheeks do coy,
> And stick musk-roses in thy sleek smooth head,
> And kiss thy fair large ears, my gentle joy.

BOTTOM *lies on stage right bench, on his back, with face slightly*
out to audience.

TITANIA *sits on the bench up by* **BOTTOM'S** *head; she places a*
flower behind his ear and kisses his big donkey ear.

BOTTOM

Where's Peas-blossom?

PEAS-BLOSSOM

Ready.

BOTTOM

Scratch my head, Peas-blossom. *(she scratches his ears; he sighs, groans, and brays with pleasure)* Where's Monsieur Cobweb?

COBWEB

Ready.

BOTTOM

Monsieur Cobweb, good monsieur, get your weapons in your hand, and kill me a red-hipp'd humble-bee on the top of a thistle; and, good monsieur, bring me the honey-bag.

Exit **COBWEB** *stage right.*

Where's Monsieur Mustard-Seed?

MUSTARD-SEED

What's your will?

BOTTOM

Nothing, good monsieur, but to help Cavalery Peas-blossom to scratch. **(MUSTARD-SEED** *scratches* **BOTTOM'S** *ear; he sighs, groans, and brays with pleasure)* I must to the barber's, monsieur; for methinks I am marvelous hairy about the face; and I am such a tender ass, if my hair do but tickle me, I must scratch.

TITANIA
>What, wilt thou hear some music, my sweet love?

BOTTOM
>I have a reasonable good ear in music: Let's have the tongs and bones.

SOUND OPERATOR plays Sound Cue #1 ("New age music").

Enter FAIRIES *from rear and dance about* BOTTOM *with scarves and wands.*

>(BOTTOM *yawns*) I have an exposition of sleep come upon me.

TITANIA
>Sleep thou, and I will wind thee in my arms.
>Fairies, be gone, and be all ways away.

Exit FAIRIES.

>O, how I love thee! How I dote on thee!

BOTTOM *and* TITANIA *sleep.*

Enter PUCK *from rear, approaching* OBERON *on his right hand side.*

OBERON (*advancing toward sleeping* TITANIA *and* BOTTOM)
>Welcome, good Robin. Seest thou this sweet sight?
>Her dotage now I do begin to pity.
>For, meeting her of late behind the wood,
>Seeking sweet favors for this hateful fool,
>I did upbraid her and fall out with her.
>For she his hairy temples then had rounded
>With coronet of fresh and fragrant flowers;
>And that same dew, which sometime on the buds

Was wont to swell like round and orient pearls,
Stood now within the pretty flouriets' eyes,
Like tears that did their own disgrace bewail.
When I had at my pleasure taunted her,
And she in mild terms begged my patience,
I then did ask of her her changeling child,
Which straight she gave me, and her fairy sent
To bear him to my bower in Fairyland.
And now I have the boy, I will undo
This hateful imperfection of her eyes.
And, gentle Puck, take this transformèd scalp
From off the head of this Athenian swain,
That he, awaking when the other do,
May all to Athens back again repair
And think no more of this night's accidents
But as the fierce vexation of a dream.
But first I will release the Fairy Queen.

OBERON *applies the nectar to her eyes.*

Be as thou wast wont to be.
See as thou wast wont to see.
Dian's bud o'er Cupid's flower
Hath such force and blessèd power.
Now, my Titania, wake you, my sweet queen.

TITANIA *(awakening, groggy, and seeing* **OBERON***)*
My Oberon! What visions have I seen!
Methought I was enamour'd of an ass.

OBERON *(pointing to* **BOTTOM***)*
There lies your love.

TITANIA *(shrieking and jumping up)*
How came these things to pass?

She runs to stage left bench away from BOTTOM.

> O, how mine eyes do loathe his visage now!
> *(turns away, shields her eyes)*

OBERON

> Silence awhile.—Robin, take off this head.—
> Titania, music call; and strike more dead
> Than common sleep of all these five the sense.

TITANIA

> Music, ho! Music, such as charmeth sleep.

SOUND OPERATOR *plays* Sound Cue #2 ("New age music").

PUCK

> Now, when thou wakest, with thine own fool's eyes
> peep.

PUCK *removes ass head from* BOTTOM, *who falls back asleep.*

TITANIA

> Come, my lord; and in our flight,
> Tell me how it came this night
> That I sleeping here was found
> With these mortals on the ground.

Exit PUCK *and* TITANIA *stage right, holding hands.*

Enter THESEUS, HIPPOLYTA, EGEUS, *and* ATTENDANT *from rear.*

THESEUS

> We will, fair queen, up to the mountain's top,
> *(sees the two couples)* But, soft! What nymphs
> are these?

EGEUS
> My lord, this is my daughter here asleep
> And this, Lysander; this Demetrius is;
> This Helena, I wonder of their being here together.

THESEUS *(to* ATTENDANT*)*
> Wake them.

ATTENDANT *shakes tambourine in couples' ears, and they wake, startled.*

LYSANDER
> Pardon, my lord. *(sitting up, sees* THESEUS *and bows*
> *clumsily from a sitting position)*

THESEUS
> I pray you all, stand up.

The two couples stand up, a little confused and nervous.

> I know you two are rival enemies:

LYSANDER *and* DEMETRIUS *look at each other as if to say, "What's up?", smile, and non-verbally congratulate each other on the other's woman.*

> How comes this gentle concord in the world,
> That hatred is so far from jealousy,
> To sleep by hate, and fear no enmity?

LYSANDER
> My lord,
> I cannot truly say how I came here;
> I came with Hermia hither *(looks at* HERMIA
> *utterly googly-eyed)*

EGEUS *(angrily, almost shouting)*
I beg the law, the law, upon his head.

DEMETRIUS
But, my good lord, I wot not by what power,—
But by some power it is,—my love to Hermia,
Melted as the snow,
And all the faith, the virtue of my heart,
The object, and the pleasure of mine eye,
Is only Helena. *(looks at* HELENA *utterly googly-eyed)*

THESEUS
Fair lovers, you are fortunately met:
Egeus, I will overbear your will;
For in the temple, by and by, with us
These couples shall eternally be knit:
Away with us to Athens! Three and three,
We'll hold a feast in great solemnity.
Come, Hippolyta.

Exit THESEUS, HIPPOLYTA, EGEUS, *and* ATTENDANT *stage left.*

DEMETRIUS *(to* HELENA*)*
Are you sure
That we are awake? It seems to me
That yet we sleep, we dream.
Let's follow him;
And, by the way, let us recount our dreams.

Exit DEMETRIUS *and* HELENA *stage left.*

BOTTOM *(waking)*
I have had a most rare vision. I have had a dream,—
past the wit of man to say what dream it was: Man
is but an ass, if he go about to expound this dream.
Methought I was *(feels his face)* and methought I

had *(feels his ears)* but man is but a patch'd fool, if he will offer to say what methought I had. I will get Peter Quince to write a ballad of this dream: It shall be called Bottom's Dream, because it hath no bottom; and I will sing it in the latter end of a play before the duke.

Exit BOTTOM *stage right.*

✳ A MIDSUMMER NIGHT'S DREAM: PERFORMANCE NOTES

I directed this production of *A Midsummer Night's Dream* in the year 2000 with a group of ninth graders. The play is colorful, fanciful, and magical, and actors have a lot of fun bringing the fantasy to life. It is important to keep the entrances and exits crisp. The stage should never be empty. I liken it to a relay race: The runner receiving the baton starts to run before he receives it. Likewise, as an actor or group of actors leaves the stage, the next group should be entering. Especially in a madcap story like this one, the pace should be quick and the energy high. It is a dream, after all, so everything that happens is beyond the realm of mortal understanding!

A MIDSUMMER NIGHT'S DREAM: ACT IV, SCENE I

When the narrator opens this scene with the words, "We are still in the woods," she looks around apprehensively, as if she is afraid of what might be lurking around her. This is a nice touch, and not only helps build a mood for the setting, but also makes the narrator part of the world we are creating. The actor playing Bottom in this production is very demanding and loud, similar to a diva—or Mick Jagger on tour. New Age music plays on the boom box as the glittery fairies dance about Bottom, who is enjoying his new status as a kind of deity.

In retrospect, I would have had this fairy dance last longer. Furthermore, I would have invited a dance choreographer from the school or from a local dance academy to design something fanciful. I hand out a questionnaire at the beginning of each project, asking students to list a few hobbies and interests. Those who mention dance are good candidates for movement-oriented roles. Their input is also valuable in choreography. Ideas and suggestions that come directly from the actors themselves are often the most valuable of all.

At the end Bottom's "dream" speech, he exits skipping. This was a choice by the actor playing Bottom, not mine as director. There is something so merry and innocent about the act of skipping. When Bottom skips offstage, he inspires the actors playing the two pairs of lovers to skip on for the following scene. It is almost as if the cast has imbibed a magical potion that causes them to skip. Simple musical instruments or noisemakers played live provide a lovely touch to any production. When the royalty enter to wake the sleeping lovers, the attendant uses a tambourine to rouse them.

For this production of A Midsummer Night's Dream, cast members also added their own creative touches to the costuming, including a lovely "wall costume" for the character of Wall. Whenever actors contribute creatively to a play, inspired performances follow.

A Midsummer Night's Dream ranks as one of William Shakespeare's most colorful and lighthearted plays. I hope that the experience of performing this comedy will bring delight and laughter to both actors and audiences alike.

✳ A MIDSUMMER NIGHT'S DREAM: MONOLOGUE NOTES

ACT IV, SCENE I: OBERON MONOLOGUE

Oberon has been working his charms on the lovers in the woods and has transformed Bottom into an ass. He has also charmed his wife Titania, the Fairy Queen, to fall in love with Bottom. Oberon's lines are spoken as he watches Titania doting on Bottom and catering to his every wish.

It appears that the sight of Titania fulfilling Bottom's desires brings a change to Oberon. Up until this point in the play, he has been enjoying the result of his spell on Bottom and Titania. He explains his change of heart to Puck in language that is at times sweet and at other times harsh.

Most of the passage—and most of *A Midsummer Night's Dream*—is written in iambic pentameter. When speaking in this rhythm, you should maintain the pulse of the pattern without making them singsong. Let the words flow out as natural sentences. Each line is not stated in perfect iambic pentameter; some lines have an extra syllable.

I like to think of the rhyme scheme of a Shakespearean passage, particularly the iambic pentameter, as a heartbeat. Sometimes the addition of an extra syllable to a line of iambic pentameter will indicate that the heartbeat of the character has become irregular as a result of an emotional change. Keep an eye out for changes in the rhythm of the speech. Do these changes correlate with a shift in the character's feeling?

Oberon's feelings in this speech are not obvious. Initially, he refers to the sight of Titania and Bottom together as "sweet." In the next line, he indicates that it is causing him "pity." Two lines later he refers to Bottom as a "hateful fool." He also uses the words "hateful imperfection" to describe Titania's eyes.

It is possible that Oberon is not being completely honest with Puck about his true feelings of the sight of Bottom and Titania together. When he tells of his encounter with Titania in the woods, he describes the flowers with which she had "rounded" Bottom's "hairy temples." He likens the dew in those flowers to "tears that did their own disgrace bewail." Maybe the flowers are Titania's eyes. Maybe the tears are Oberon's. Perhaps the disgrace is Oberon's. As an actor, you have the opportunity to explore these metaphors and personalize them to your character and his feelings.

As with every monologue, you should choose specific words to color and emphasize. Does Oberon's voice rise with anger on words such as "hateful"? Does his voice fall with pity or sadness on "disgrace bewail?" Lend the words and passages emotional power by using your face and body to illustrate them. Likewise, when describing the flowers, employ soft gestures to help the audience envision the flowers. When saying the words "fresh and fragrant," you can smell the flowers, smell the air, or simply close your eyes and imagine their smell.

In the final lines before Oberon releases Titania from his spell, he vows to "think no more of this night's accidents / But as the fierce vexation of a dream." Throughout the play, even in the title itself, there arises the question of what is real and what is a spell or a dream. In this case, by casting a spell on Titania and Bottom and observing the resulting affection Titania displays toward the ass, perhaps Oberon does not merely pity Titania. He might be jealous as well. Play around with this dynamic. Try the passage with a dominant emotion of jealousy. Try it with more pity. Experiment with anger and with sweetness. See what the words themselves evoke in your representation of your character. It is possible that your interpretation will include some of each of these emotions. As always, mine the text for hints as to how your character feels. Let the words themselves dictate your feelings.

Remember that Oberon is talking to Puck in this scene. You can talk to the actor playing Puck on the stage, or if you are performing the monologue solo, you can speak to an imaginary Puck. Either way, when describing his encounter with Titania in the woods, Oberon can imagine that in his mind's eye, and take the audience with him on his descriptive journey. When beginning his remembrance, Oberon might tilt his head back a little or unfocus his eyes to indicate that he is recalling that moment in time. Sometimes a small physical shift can go far toward creating a mood.

For the last lines of the monologue, Oberon speaks directly to the sleeping Titania. Look at Titania, and let your eyes show your feelings for your wife. Even though Oberon and Titania are fairies, they possess distinctly human qualities and feelings of anger, sorrow, jealousy, and ultimately love. This is, after all a Shakespearean comedy, and so love must conquer all. Let that feeling ring in your voice as you close the speech with these words: "Now, my Titania, wake you, my sweet queen."

SUGGESTED VIEWING

A MIDSUMMER NIGHT'S DREAM, 1935
Directors: William Dieterle, Max Reinhardt
Starring: Ian Hunter, Olivia DeHavilland, James Cagney, Mickey Rooney

A MIDSUMMER NIGHT'S DREAM, 1968
Director: Peter Hall
Starring: Ian Richardson, Judi Dench, Helen Mirren

✳ MUCH ADO ABOUT NOTHING

CHARACTERS IN THE PLAY

The following is a list of characters that appear in this scene of
Much Ado About Nothing.

BENEDICK: A young lord of Padua
DON PEDRO: Prince of Aragon
CLAUDIO: A young lord of Florence
LEONATO: Governor of Messina
NARRATOR

SET AND PROP LIST

SET PIECES:
Bench
Potted plant, large enough for Benedick to hide behind

✳ *MUCH ADO ABOUT NOTHING:*
ACT II, SCENE III

Leonato's orchard.

Enter NARRATOR *from rear, coming downstage center.*

NARRATOR
>Benedick declares that he will never love one
>woman; The three men trick Benedick into believing
>Beatrice loves him. Benedick falls for it and decides
>to love Beatrice.

Exit NARRATOR *stage left.*

Enter BENEDICK *from stage right and walks downstage center.*

BENEDICK
>Love may transform me to an oyster; but I'll take
>my oath on it, till he have made an oyster of me, he
>shall never make me a fool. One woman is fair, yet
>I am well; another is wise, yet I am well; another
>virtuous, yet I am well; but till all graces be in one
>woman, one woman shall not come in my grace.
>Ha! The prince and Monsieur Love! I will hide me
>in the arbor.

BENEDICK *hides behind stage left pillar.*

Enter DON PEDRO, CLAUDIO, *and* LEONATO. *They stand downstage center.*

DON PEDRO

See you where Benedick hath hid himself?
(louder, so that BENEDICK *hears)*
Come hither, Leonato. What was it you told me of
to-day, that your niece Beatrice was in love with
Signior Benedick?

Hiding behind a plant, BENEDICK *starts to inch toward the
others, until plant is to the right of the bench.*

CLAUDIO

I did never think that lady would have loved any
man.

LEONATO

No, nor I neither; but most wonderful that she
should so dote on Signior Benedick, whom she hath
in all outward behaviors seemed ever to abhor.

BENEDICK *(pops his head up from behind plant)*
Is't possible? Sits the wind in that corner?

DON PEDRO

Why, what effects of passion shows she?

CLAUDIO

Bait the hook well; this fish will bite.

CLAUDIO *starts to walk left, in front of plant and bench, and
the others follow.* DON PEDRO, LEONATO, *and* CLAUDIO *all sit
on bench.*

DON PEDRO

How, how, pray you? You amaze me: I would have
I thought her spirit had been invincible against all
assaults of affection.

LEONATO

> I would have sworn it had, my lord; especially
> against Benedick.

BENEDICK *(from behind plant, head popping up)*

> I should think this a gull, but that the white-bearded
> fellow speaks it: Knavery cannot, sure, hide himself
> in such reverence.

BENEDICK *sees others looking toward him and pops his head
back down quickly.*

CLAUDIO

> He hath ta'en the infection: Hold it up.

*The three men stand up and start walking stage right, in front of
pillar, just to bother* **BENEDICK** *and make him follow.*

DON PEDRO

> Hath she made her affection known to Benedick?

LEONATO

> No; and swears she never will: That's her torment.

BENEDICK, *frustrated at not being able to hear, starts crawling
out from behind plant and tries to get behind stage right pillar.*

LEONATO

> She'll be up twenty times a night, and there will she
> sit in her smock till she have writ a sheet of paper:
> My daughter tells us all.

CLAUDIO

> Now you talk of a sheet of paper, I remember a
> pretty jest your daughter told us of.

LEONATO

> O, when she had writ it and was reading it over, she found Benedick and Beatrice between the sheet?

BENEDICK *stops mid-crawl. Others look over, so* BENEDICK, *center stage, pretends he is a bench.*

LEONATO

> O, she tore the letter into a thousand halfpence; railed at herself, that she should be so immodest to write to one that she knew would flout her.

CLAUDIO

> Then down upon her knees she falls, weeps, sobs, beats her heart, tears her hair, prays, curses; "O sweet Benedick! God give me patience!"

CLAUDIO *walks over to* BENEDICK *(still as a bench) and sits on his back.* BENEDICK *reacts to strain with facial expressions.*

DON PEDRO

> It were good that Benedick knew of it by some other, if she will not discover it.

DON PEDRO *also sits on* BENEDICK, *who reacts to the increased strain.*

CLAUDIO

> To what end? He would make but a sport of it and torment the poor lady worse.

DON PEDRO

> If she should make tender of her love, 'tis very possible he'll scorn it; for the man, as you know all, hath a contemptible spirit. I am sorry for your niece. Shall we go seek Benedick, and tell him of her love?

CLAUDIO

> Never tell him, my lord: Let her wear it out with good counsel.

LEONATO

> Nay, that's impossible: She may wear her heart out first.

LEONATO sits on BENEDICK *as well.* BENEDICK *can barely hold them.*

DON PEDRO

> Well, we will hear further of it by your daughter: Let it cool the while. I love Benedick well; and I could wish he would modestly examine himself, to see how much he is unworthy so good a lady.

LEONATO

> My lord, will you walk? Dinner is ready.

DON PEDRO

> Let there be the same net spread for her.

Exit DON PEDRO, CLAUDIO, *and* LEONATO *stage right.*

BENEDICK *(coming forward)*

> This can be no trick. The conference was sadly borne; they have the truth of this from Hero; they seem to pity the lady. It seems her affections have their full bent. Love me? Why, it must be requited! I hear how I am censured. They say I will bear myself proudly if I perceive the love come from her. They say, too, that she will rather die than give any sign of affection. I did never think to marry. I must not seem proud. Happy are they that hear their detractions and can put them to mending. They say the lady is fair; 'tis a truth, I

can bear them witness. And virtuous; 'tis so, I cannot reprove it. And wise, but for loving me; by my troth, it is no addition to her wit, nor no great argument of her folly, for I will be horribly in love with her! I may chance have some odd quirks and remnants of wit broken on me because I have railed so long against marriage, but doth not the appetite alter? A man loves the meat in his youth that he cannot endure in his age. Shall quips and sentences and these paper bullets of the brain awe a man from the career of his humor? No! The world must be peopled. When I said I would die a bachelor, I did not think I should live till I were married. Here comes Beatrice. By this day, she's a fair lady. I do spy some marks of love in her.

Exit **BENEDICK** *stage right.*

✳ MUCH ADO ABOUT NOTHING: PERFORMANCE NOTES

I directed this performance of *Much Ado About Nothing* in 2006. This production consisted of a group of twenty-five ninth graders— and only one male! In the middle of the rehearsal period, when I asked the student (who played Benedick) how he was holding up, he grinned widely and responded, "I'm lovin' it!" If only all ninth graders could have that kind of positive attitude. Although my 2006 production included only one male actor, the plot and relationships were believable because the actors committed themselves. A couple of fake beards for Don John and Leonato, applied with spirit gum, can help perpetuate the illusion of maleness. Most of this illusion can be achieved through actors' dedication to their roles and their relationships.

This comedy is characterized by the fun battle of words between Beatrice and Benedick and by the hysterical pranks played on the lovers by their peers. But what gives the script its punch is its flip side: the brutal rejection of Hero by her groom at the altar and the subsequent ruse (faking her own death) and redemption (Claudio marrying the "substitute" Hero) that follow.

What gives the best comedies their power is often the pain that lurks behind the surface and under the laughter. Such is also the case with the battles between Beatrice and Benedick. Their war of words is amusing, but both have been hurt in love, and the clever verbal barbs they direct at each other are their armor. It is clear from their words that they have a history, and it is not a pretty one. I encourage the actors to play the "word fight" scenes for laughs, but to be aware of the history of hurt that underlies their words and undercuts the humor, ironically making it funnier. How do they achieve this subtlety? Often simply being aware of this nuance, which is readily uncovered by mining the text, is sufficient to allow the actors to give their characters some weight. And it is this weight that makes the lightness lighter! I dwell on this point because it is an important one that can be successfully applied to all comedies.

The stage directions have actors entering from the rear of the stage. These scenes were designed for the Folger Shakespeare Library's Elizabethan stage, which often has a rear entrance for actors. This direction has the advantage of varying the entrances, but it can result in actors "clumping" upstage and not descending far enough downstage to be properly visible and audible to the audience. Over the years, I have tended to scale back "rear entrances," and since there is no guarantee that your performance space will have an available entrance at the rear of the stage, please feel free to use side entrances exclusively.

Having said that, if there is an opportunity at some point for an actor to enter from the rear of the audience, this can be an effective and fun way to shake things up while breaking the "third wall." Audiences love being physically close to actors, and if there is an opportunity for a player entering from the audience to somehow interact with someone in the seats (a directed comment, eye contact, etc.) this audience entrance gives us that opportunity. In *Much Ado About Nothing*, Don John is a villain, and therefore it would be not out of character for him to purposefully glare or even menace an audience member for his own delight, which has the added advantage of accentuating his evil nature.

During the performance of this version of *Much Ado About Nothing*, a "situation" occurred at the beginning of the third scene. The stage was bare, and no actors were forthcoming. The actress playing the sound cues on the boom box was sitting on the side of stage right, unaware that it was her cue to rise and deliver the narrator's lines center stage to begin the scene. Nobody backstage was prompting her, and the stage was likely going to remain vacant for some time, so I prompted the actor from my seat in the audience. The scenario was not ideal, but it was far preferable to the void that was facing us at that moment. Castmates and crew members should be ready to step in and come to the rescue if necessary. Over the years I have increased my emphasis on actors preparing to help from backstage, with a stage manager and various assistants, whose job it is to keep track of cues, props, entrances, and exits, and to intervene when needed. I post "cue cheat sheets" with the cues that precede actors' entrances, and I leave plenty of scripts backstage.

MUCH ADO ABOUT NOTHING: ACT II, SCENE III

This scene should be fun and funny. The humor works best if the hiding Benedick does is in plain view of the conspirators, who should make it clear to the audience that they do indeed see him, but choose not to acknowledge it for the sake of their ruse. When Benedick hides behind the potted plant and tiptoes gradually toward the group, his legs should stick out at the bottom, his head should poke out from the top, and his tiptoeing should be large and exaggerated. When Benedick crawls out from behind the plant, ending up on all fours behind the trio, they may then sit on him as if he is a bench. This is, of course, absurd, since any sentient being would be able to discern that he is sitting on a human being, but therein lies the comedy. To heighten the absurdity, Benedick himself may non-verbally express shock and amazement that he is not caught. The blocking indicates that all three actors sit on Benedick simultaneously, but the comedy works well (and might be easier on the poor actor playing Benedick) if only one person sits on him, while the others pretend that they are about to sit, which terrifies Benedick, and then change their minds, which relieves him! It is also very comical if, while he is being sat upon, Benedick makes little grunting sounds.

When Claudio imitates Beatrice with the line, "O, sweet Benedick, God give me patience," he will get a laugh if he uses a goofy, high-pitched parody vocal rather than his own voice.

As the three plotters walk off the stage, Benedick remains on all fours with his buttocks up in the air, and his head and back down on the stage as if he has been crushed. This scene provides a great opportunity to achieve big laughs with few props or costume gimmicks, just dialogue and bodies.

The humor works on two levels, verbal and physical, and it is best to separate the two. The collaborator sits on Benedick. Actors allow the audience's laughter to subside, and then speak their lines. Novice actors frequently step on their own laughter by reciting the next lines too soon, which not only diminishes the reaction but also prohibits the audience from hearing the dialogue.

For Benedick's final line of the scene ("The world must be peopled"), I asked him to accompany the phrase with a gesture of his choice. Ultimately he chose to stick his fist up in the air with arm outstretched, an action that my generation associates with the "Black Power" salute. The ninth grade actor who played Benedick was African American, and I did not ask him why he chose that move, but it got a laugh. Many of the most satisfying laughs arrive at otherwise dramatic and poignant moments. The audience has no problem switching gears emotionally, and they may immediately re-enter back into the drama, grateful for a laugh to relieve the tension. What is interesting is how one motion can impart an interesting and perhaps unexpected interpretation.

In the final scene, when Beatrice and Benedick finally embrace each other, the entire audience of adolescents and adults responded with a spontaneous "Awww." We were ready for the couple to get together. We cared. We believed in the story and had been swept away by its poetic protagonists. That is the magic of Shakespeare. May it be your magic, too.

✳ *MUCH ADO ABOUT NOTHING:* MONOLOGUE NOTES

ACT II, SCENE III: BENEDICK MONOLOGUE

This monologue has the perfect opening line: "This can be no trick." Why is it perfect? Because we the audience know the exact opposite to be true. We have information that Benedick does not. As Benedick, you would do well to speak to the audience and to do so with absolute confidence. The more confident you are in your version of the truth, the more we as audience members will howl with laughter at your delusions.

Benedick believes he speaks the truth in part because the information about Beatrice loving him supposedly came from Hero, a very trustworthy person. When you say her name, "Hero," say it as if the name itself is a guarantee of truth.

As an experiment with the line "Love me?", try saying the line with an exclamation point instead of a question mark: "Love me!" You as the actor have some poetic license here. What physical gesture accompanies these two words? Does Benedick stretch his arms heavenward? Does he hug himself? Or does he leap up and click his heels together? Take a video of yourself delivering these two words in three different ways.

Let the passion burn through your eyes on the line "Why, it must be requited!" The idea that Beatrice loves him has awakened a side of Benedick that we have never seen. Prior to this scene, he has been playfully sarcastic. Now a romantic and giddy Benedick emerges. Make sure to identify Benedick's dominant emotion on the line

"They say, too, that she will rather die than give any sign of affection." Could he be genuinely moved and flattered? Or is it more of a revelation, explaining her cold behavior to him up until this point?

Find the points in the speech where Benedick attempts to curb his own enthusiasm: "I must not seem proud." This line can be delivered in a more purposefully somber manner than the previous breathless exclamations. Perhaps Benedick breathes deeply and makes a hand gesture to indicate that he is attempting to calm himself.

Benedick proceeds to list some of Beatrice's qualities: "fair," "virtuous," and "wise." You can color each of these descriptive words to give them more dramatic power. Picture a person with these fine qualities in your mind's eye, and frame each word with a hand gesture or a slight beat, also known as a pause.

Benedick's familiar sarcasm, which has been overtaken by passion in this monologue, returns with the line "And wise, but for loving me." It is a nice self-deprecating moment of self-awareness that might be accompanied by a chuckle. He uses an interesting choice of words in the line, "I will be horribly in love with her." Benedick uses the following words to describe his own way of behaving: "odd quirks," "remnants of wit," "railed," and "paper bullets." Much of what you might need to know about Benedick is revealed in his own self-description.

Benedick seems to be listing reasons for him to love Beatrice: 1) She loves him, 2) she has good qualities, 3) his "appetite" has altered, and finally, 4) "the world must be peopled." This final reason can be spoken with a grandiosity that befits the responsibility Benedick seems to feel to carry on the species. Make this statement big and funny!

Finally, Benedick explains, "When I said I would die a bachelor, I did not think I would live till I were married." As an actor and a comedian, you have an opportunity to let the odd logic of this sink in with your portrayal of the character. Think about it, and try pausing before "till I were married" as if you are trying to have your words make sense, even though you don't know what you will be saying until you are saying it. Exploit the comedy of these words with funny pauses, gestures, and facial expressions to accompany Benedick's emotions.

When Benedick finally sees Beatrice at the end of the speech, what is his emotional response? Excitement? Nervousness? Surprise? Fear? Experiment with different dominant emotions before deciding on an approach, always letting the words in the text provide you with clues on how to play the monologue.

Benedick is at times loud and effusive, and at other moments more quiet and thoughtful. Find the dynamics in this speech and have fun with it. The audience will laugh with you.

SUGGESTED VIEWING

MUCH ADO ABOUT NOTHING, 1993
Director: Kenneth Branagh
Starring: Kenneth Branagh, Emma Thompson, Keanu Reeves, Kate Beckinsale

MUCH ADO ABOUT NOTHING, 2012
Director: Joss Whedon
Starring: Alexis Denisof, Amy Acker

✳ OTHELLO

CHARACTERS IN THE PLAY

The following is a list of characters that appear in this scene of Othello.

OTHELLO
DESDEMONA: Wife to Othello
CASSIO: An honorable lieutenant
IAGO: An ensign and villain
RODERIGO: A gullible gentleman trying to woo Desdemona
MONTANO: Governor of Cypress
SOLDIERS
NARRATOR

SET AND PROP LIST

SET PIECES:
Bench
Two chairs
Table

PROPS:
Flask for Iago
Goblets and wine bottles for soldiers
Swords for soldiers

✳ *OTHELLO:* ACT II, SCENE III

Cyprus. A hall in the castle.

Enter NARRATOR *from stage rear, coming downstage center.*

NARRATOR
> We are now in Cyprus. Iago persuades Cassio to drink too much, which is part of Iago's devious plan of action.

Exit NARRATOR *stage left.*

Enter OTHELLO *and* DESDEMONA *from stage rear. Enter* CASSIO *from stage right.*

OTHELLO *(to* CASSIO*)*
> Good Michael, look you to the guard to-night:
> Good night.

Exit OTHELLO *and* DESDEMONA *stage rear.*

Enter IAGO *from stage right, carrying a flask.*

CASSIO
> Welcome, Iago; we must to the watch.

IAGO
> Come, lieutenant, I have a stoup of wine; to the health of black Othello.

CASSIO

> Not to-night, good Iago: I have very poor and
> unhappy brains for drinking.

IAGO

> What, man! 'Tis a night of revels: the gallants
> desire it.

CASSIO

> I'll do't; but it dislikes me.

IAGO *(steps downstage; addresses audience)*

> If I can fasten but one cup upon him,
> He'll be as full of quarrel and offense
> As my young mistress' dog.

Enter **RODERIGO, MONTANO,** *and* **SOLDIERS** *from stage right,*
holding goblets, with an extra for **CASSIO.**

CASSIO

> To the health of our general!

ALL *drink.* **CASSIO** *drinks quickly and refills his cup.*

MONTANO

> I am for it, lieutenant; and I'll do you justice.

IAGO

> O sweet England!

ALL *(singing)*

> And let me the cannikin clink, clink
> And let me the cannikin clink.
> A soldier's a man,
> O man's life's but a span,

Why, then let a soldier drink
Why, then let a soldier drink!

IAGO

Some wine, ho!

CASSIO *(pours more wine for himself)*
Why, this is a more exquisite song than the other.
Do not think, gentlemen. I am drunk: This is my
ancient; this is my right hand, and this is my left:
I am not drunk now; I can stand well enough, and
speak well enough.

Exit CASSIO *stage left.*

IAGO *(aside, to* RODERIGO*)*
How now, Roderigo!
I pray you, after the lieutenant; go.

Exit RODERIGO *stage left.*

RODERIGO *(from offstage)*
Help! Help!

Enter RODERIGO, *chased by* CASSIO.

CASSIO
'Zounds, you rogue! You rascal!
A knave teach me my duty! *(strikes* RODERIGO*)*

MONTANO
Nay, good lieutenant; I pray you, sir, hold your hand.

CASSIO
Let me go, sir, or I'll knock you o'er the mazard.

MONTANO
Come, come, you're drunk.

CASSIO
Drunk!

CASSIO *and* MONTANO *fight;* MONTANO *is injured.*

IAGO *(aside, to* RODERIGO*)*
Away, I say, go out; and cry a mutiny!

Exit RODERIGO *stage rear.*

SOUND OPERATOR *plays* Sound Cue #1 ("Ringing bell").

Enter OTHELLO *and* DESDEMONA *from stage rear.*

OTHELLO
What is the matter here?
Are we turn'd Turks? Honest Iago,
Speak, who began this?

IAGO
I had rather have this tongue cut from my mouth
Than it should do offense to Michael Cassio;
But men are men; the best sometimes forget.

OTHELLO
I know, Iago,
Thy honesty and love doth mince this matter,
Making it light to Cassio. Cassio, I love thee;
But never more be officer of mine.

Exit OTHELLO *and* DESDEMONA *stage rear. Exit* ALL *but* IAGO *and*
CASSIO *stage right.*

CASSIO *(falls to his knees)*
> Reputation, reputation, reputation! O, I have lost my reputation! I have lost the immortal part of myself, and what remains is bestial.

IAGO *(helps* CASSIO *to his feet)*
> As I am an honest man, I'll tell you what you shall do. Our general's wife is now the general: Confess yourself freely to her; importune her help to put you in your place again.

CASSIO
> You advise me well. In the morning I will beseech the virtuous Desdemona to undertake for me: Good night, honest Iago.

Exit CASSIO *stage right.*

IAGO
> And what's he, then, that says I play the villain,
> When this advice is free I give and honest,
> Probal to thinking, and indeed the course
> To win the Moor again? For 'tis most easy
> Th' inclining Desdemona to subdue
> In any honest suit. She's framed as fruitful
> As the free elements. And then for her
> To win the Moor—were 't to renounce his baptism,
> All seals and symbols of redeemèd sin—
> His soul is so enfettered to her love
> That she may make, unmake, do what she list,
> Even as her appetite shall play the god
> With his weak function. How am I then a villain
> To counsel Cassio to this parallel course
> Directly to his good? Divinity of hell!
> When devils will the blackest sins put on,
> They do suggest at first with heavenly shows,

As I do now. For whiles this honest fool
Plies Desdemona to repair his fortune,
And she for him pleads strongly to the Moor,
I'll pour this pestilence into his ear:
That she repeals him for her body's lust;
And by how much she strives to do him good,
She shall undo her credit with the Moor.
So will I turn her virtue into pitch,
And out of her own goodness make the net
That shall enmesh them all.

Exit IAGO *stage right.*

✳ *OTHELLO:* PERFORMANCE NOTES

I directed this performance of *Othello* in 2002 with a Washington, D.C. public school ninth grade English class. In our production, a ninth grade young lady with a loud voice and expressive body language played Iago. An African American ninth grader played Othello. He was short for his age, but large in talent and heart. This young actor had a way of speaking the words to bring out their full color. To achieve this, a player must appreciate the sound and feeling of the words as they leave his mouth: "noble," "approved," "masters," "rude," "speech," "bless'd," "soft," "phrase," "peace." Each of these words alone is expressive, and when spoken as part of a line of Shakespeare, they are poetical.

How does one speak "poetically"? The first rule is not to rush the words. Many actors hurry their lines, which is confusing for the audience. Writing down beats and breathing points in the script helps to slow you down. Mark a slash in your text at appropriate breathing points. You can also underline words or syllables that are accentuated, and then experiment with changing the emphasis to hear how this changes a line's meaning. You can also practice "coloring" your words, or thinking of the word as not just a word, but also an emotion evoker. See if the word becomes a poem in itself, with richness that echoes its sentiment or if it enhances the image it arouses. Marking beats and coloring words will encourage you to slow down your speech.

Simple staging choices can clarify story lines and character relationships. Brabantio turns his back on Desdemona and the audience after the line, "I am glad at soul I have no other children." This is a powerful blocking choice. Actors must be careful to say their lines first, and then turn their backs to the audience; otherwise they will not be heard.

Iago's public demeanor is calm and measured, in stark contrast to his private outbursts. The more genteelly Iago plays his public persona, the more striking will be his private fits of rage and hatred. To explore this dynamic, experiment in rehearsal, exaggerating both ends of the emotional spectrum between friendly and furious. Stretch your range of expression farther than you have gone before. There is a great range of possibilities and we often don't know what the scope is until we experiment with stretching our limits. This applies not just to vocals, but also to speech combined with movement.

At the beginning of Act III, Scene IV, the narrator explains that Desdemona wants to talk to Othello about Cassio. Then she pauses, and adds, "Not a good idea." This gets a big laugh. There is not much comic relief in *Othello*. The narrator breaks the tension here, updating the audience on the story while garnering some laughter. The more serious the situation, the louder the laughter. In any tragedy, I recommend inserting a couple of moments of comic relief. The audience needs it!

OTHELLO: ACT II, SCENE III

The entrance of roughhousing soldiers sets the tone for this scene. They clink their mugs and goblets and laugh loudly, singing out of tune. Cassio, in his drunken state, drapes his arm around Iago— ironic, since Iago is about to orchestrate Cassio's downfall. Playing drunk is tricky. Many actors simply stumble about and slur their words. This Cassio does quite the opposite: He over-enunciates to compensate for his inebriation. His efforts to appear sober paint a compelling picture of drunkenness. Interestingly, this mirrors Iago's own over-friendly appearance, which he uses to mask his malevolent inner self. By showing outwardly what we are not, we reveal who we really are. Cassio's true drunkenness manifests itself quickly, as he suddenly falls ill and rushes offstage, presumably toward the bathroom, which garners a big audience response.

When Montano and Cassio return to fight, make sure to choreograph the fight scene carefully. If you don't have the tools yourself, get help from someone who can safely stage a fight. Particularly with "drunken" brawlers, it is important to keep the moves clean in order to prevent injuries. A slow-motion fight can be a safe and theatrical way to deal with fisticuffs.

When Cassio falls to his knees on the line, "Reputation, reputation, reputation!" Iago helps him up. Throughout the play, we use staging that depicts Cassio as a solid, honest, comforting friend, putting his arm around the shoulders of the same people he is deceiving. This reinforces the text and paints a fine theatrical portrait of a master liar. Iago himself, and we the audience through Cassio's asides, know the extent of his scheming, but others in the play do not have our information. Audiences love to be in on a secret. And this secret grows, creating a marvelous dramatic tension that builds until the spectators can hardly stand it.

Iago frequently addresses the audience directly. In our 2002 performance, the ninth grade young man playing Iago in this scene took great joy in his own game of deception and betrayal. He gave a little laugh while describing Cassio as an "honest fool." Often the difference between a good performance and a great one lies in the small details an actor injects into his role. In this scene, Iago's little laugh added a dimension to his personality that gave audiences that much more reason to love hating him.

By emphasizing and coloring key words, Iago punches up his speech: "So will I turn her virtue into pitch." When he speaks the line, Iago's voice rises on the word "pitch." Experiment with putting the stress on different words in the speech to elicit changes in interpretation. What if the emphasis is on the word "I"? There are so many evocative words in this speech, worthy of an actor's word-coloring skills: "honest," "fool," "repair," "fortunes," "she," "pleads," "strongly," "Moor," "pour," "pestilence," "ear," "repeals," "body's," "lust," "goodness," "net," and "enmesh." The speech is a verbal smorgasbord of images that a player can prepare for a hungry audience by coloring the words.

How do words touch characters and cause them to feel something? When Iago says the word "Moor," he has a different emotional response than Desdemona does when she speaks it. Find your character's associations with words and use them to change vocal pitch, tone, and inflection. Language is like music. In theater, if you speak the words with emotional resonance, audiences will feel it.

One way to achieve the full power of the words is through judicious use of pauses. Iago speaks his line like this: "And out of her goodness make the net that shall enmesh (pause) them all." During this pause, the audience has a chance to ask itself this question: "Whom will Iago enmesh in the net?" His answer arrives immediately: "Them all." The pause itself allows the audience to form a question they might not have asked if Iago had just hurried through the line. Do not rush these great Shakespearean passages. Languish in them. Roll the words around in your mouth like a fine wine, and then spit them out!

Thus a ninth grade English class from a D.C. public school performs one of Shakespeare's greatest tragedies, *Othello* I was proud of the way this inexperienced group immersed themselves into Shakespeare's dramatic language, and delivered the play with passion, emotion, and understanding. May this be your story, too.

✳ *OTHELLO:* MONOLOGUE NOTES

ACT II, SCENE III: IAGO MONOLOGUE

This monologue brilliantly depicts the paradox that is Iago. Though he is described by others as "honest," the only time that Iago is in fact truthful is when he speaks directly to us, the audience. Then, he is indeed brutally candid.

Iago's first line is a question: "And what's he, then, that says I play the villain?" Note the use of the word "play," as if Iago is stepping out of his world and into ours, the world of the play. Iago's talents as a puppet master may be so strong as to transcend the boundaries established by the drama: He can join our world, too. You as the actor can use Iago's words to enter the audience's world as well. See what happens when you use your own personal charm to woo the audience playfully.

Iago's speech is full of opposites. The positive qualities that other characters possess—Desdemona's helpfulness, Othello's love, Cassio's honesty—become liabilities, traits that Iago can use to poison Othello against Desdemona. Iago himself uses the word "honest" three times in this speech, first to describe his own advice and then to describe Cassio's entreaty and his nature.

Since Iago considers virtuous qualities as easy prey for his malicious intents, try vocally drawing out the vowels in the words that describe virtue and then color those words with sarcastic contempt: "honest," "fruitful," "love," and "goodness." Having delivered those words with sarcasm, now experiment with trying a different approach for the speech. Perhaps you can use a more conspiring tone, as if you are mentally putting together the pieces of a puzzle, and these traits in others are simply providing clues to help you win the game.

Therein lies the paradox of Iago. He is both an emotionless plotter and a feeling villain, one who "hates" the Moor and who sees himself as having suffered dual indignities of supposed marital infidelity at the hands of Othello and being passed over for promotion. In a prior speech at the conclusion of Act I, Scene III, Iago admits that he does not know whether this infidelity is true, but "for mere suspicion in that kind, will do as if for surety."

In fact, this act of treating a suspicion as a fact is exactly what Iago wishes Othello to do in his jealousy of Desdemona. Iago here shows a self-knowledge that he uses against others whom he assumes share his weaknesses. In order to play this speech well, you must have knowledge of Iago's previous words and deeds in the play.

Twice Iago refers to himself as being seen as a "villain." However, others frequently describe him as an "honest" man. Who is calling Iago a villain? Nobody, except for Iago himself. The monologue shifts on the following line: "Divinity of hell!" No longer is Cassio describing his plot. He is now justifying it. Furthermore, he compares himself to a devil in no uncertain terms. Of all Shakespeare's characters, Iago may be the most overtly evil.

As the actor playing Iago, it is important to recall how positively other characters in the play see you and let some of that charm influence your portrayal of this evil man. Find places in the speech where you can revel in your own malice and bring the audience in to your diabolical plan. When Iago exclaims, "I'll pour this pestilence in his ear," your eyes might widen with amazement at your own cleverness as you pantomime a pouring motion.

Find places in the speech to pause, and look for words to emphasize. These words might be consecutive; for example, on "body's lust," both "body" and "lust" can be stressed with a slight pause between them. With long speeches, you will need to break up the text and identify beats and breathing points. You will also want to look for places where the tone shifts or the emotion changes.

Since the speech is so full of opposites, you may wish to capitalize on that by using hand motions or other gestures to describe these dualities. On "divinity of hell," you could point or look up and then down. Likewise, on "turn her virtue into pitch," perhaps you can extend your open right hand on the word "virtue" and close your left hand into a fist on the word "pitch." Also consider coloring your words with descriptive emotional tones. Even something as simple as emphasizing the "t" sound in "lust" can have a great impact on imparting a feeling to a word.

Iago uses human goodness as a tool to carry out his evil desires. In doing so, he coaxes evil deeds from good people. Amazingly, he does so almost entirely with words alone. Enjoy your portrayal of one of Shakespeare's finest villains.

SUGGESTED VIEWING

OTHELLO, 1965
Director: Stuart Burge
Starring: Laurence Olivier, Frank Finlay, Derek Jacobi, Maggie Smith

OTHELLO, 1995
Director: Oliver Parker
Starring Laurence Fishburne, Kenneth Branagh, Irene Jacob

✳ ROMEO AND JULIET

CHARACTERS IN THE PLAY

The following is a list of characters that appear in this scene of
Romeo and Juliet.

ROMEO: Montague's son
JULIET: Capulet's daughter
NURSE: Juliet's nursemaid
LADY CAPULET: Capulet's wife, Juliet's mother
CAPULET: Juliet's father, feuding with Montague family
NARRATOR

SET AND PROP LIST

SET PIECES:
Bench or bed
Window

PROPS:
Pillows and sheets for bed

✳ *ROMEO AND JULIET:* ACT III, SCENE V

Capulet's home.

NARRATOR *enters from stage rear.*

ROMEO *and* **JULIET** *enter simultaneously from stage left and take their positions;* **ROMEO** *sits on right, in front of bench, and* **JULIET** *lies on bench, sleeping.*

NARRATOR

> Romeo and Juliet are secretly married by Friar Lawrence, but their joy does not last long. As Romeo tries to break up a fight, Juliet's cousin Tybalt kills Romeo's friend Mercutio. In revenge, Romeo kills Tybalt, and the Prince banishes Romeo from Verona. Romeo and Juliet spend their wedding night together, but must leave each other at dawn.

Exit **NARRATOR** *stage left.*

JULIET *(awakens and sees* **ROMEO***)*

> Wilt thou be gone? It is not yet near day:
> It was the nightingale, and not the lark,
> That pierced the fearful hollow of thine ear.

ROMEO

> It was the lark, the herald of the morn,
> I must be gone and live, or stay and die.

JULIET

> Hie hence, be gone, away!

It is the lark that sings so out of tune,
More light and light it grows.

ROMEO

More light and light; more dark and dark our woes!

Enter **NURSE** *from stage rear.*

NURSE *(in a panic)*

Madam!

JULIET

Nurse?

NURSE

Your lady mother is coming to your chamber:
The day is broke; be wary, look about.

Exit **NURSE** *stage rear.*

JULIET

Then, window, let day in, and let life out.
(opens window while facing audience)

ROMEO

Farewell, farewell! One kiss, and I'll descend.

They kiss. **ROMEO** *crosses down stage right.*

JULIET *(frightened, upset)*

O God, I have an ill-divining soul!
Methinks I see thee, now thou art below,
As one dead in the bottom of a tomb:
Either my eyesight fails, or thou look'st pale.

ROMEO *(responding, but still cheating out)*
>And trust me, love, in my eye so do you:
>Dry sorrow drinks our blood. Adieu, adieu!

Exit ROMEO *stage right.*

JULIET *(straight out to audience)*
>O fortune, fortune! All men call thee fickle:
>Be fickle, fortune;
>For then, I hope, thou wilt not keep him long,
>But send him back.

LADY CAPULET *(from within, stage rear)*
>Ho, daughter! Are you up?

JULIET
>Who is't that calls? Is it my lady mother?

Enter LADY CAPULET *from stage rear.*

LADY CAPULET
>Why, how now, Juliet!

JULIET *(turns away from her, stage right)*
>Madam, I am not well.

LADY CAPULET *(comforts* JULIET, *tentatively putting a hand on her shoulder)*
>Evermore weeping for your cousin's death?
>What, wilt thou wash him from his grave with tears?
>But now I'll tell thee joyful tidings, girl.

JULIET *turns, interested.*

>Early next Thursday morn,
>The gallant, young, and noble gentleman,

The County Paris, at Saint Peter's Church,
Shall happily make thee there a joyful bride.

JULIET *(tears herself away, backing up stage right)*
He shall not make me there a joyful bride.
I will not marry yet; and, when I do, I swear,
It shall be Romeo, whom you know I hate,
Rather than Paris.

LADY CAPULET
Here comes your father; tell him so yourself.

LADY CAPULET *moves stage left.*

Enter **CAPULET** *and* **NURSE** *from stage rear.*

NURSE *stands stage right behind* **JULIET**, **LADY CAPULET** *stage left.* **JULIET** *and* **CAPULET** *stand center, with* **JULIET** *to stage right of* **CAPULET**.

CAPULET
How now! A conduit, girl? What, still in tears?
How now, wife!
Have you deliver'd to her our decree?

LADY CAPULET
Ay, sir; but she will none, she gives you thanks.
I would the fool were married to her grave!

CAPULET *(astounded, center stage)*
(to **LADY CAPULET***)* How! Doth she not give
us thanks?
Unworthy as she is, that we have wrought
So worthy a gentleman to be her bridegroom?

JULIET *(standing up to* CAPULET*)*
> Proud can I never be of what I hate.

CAPULET
> What is this? *(turns and approaches* JULIET
> *menacingly; she shrinks away)*
> Fettle your fine joints 'gainst Thursday next,
> To go with Paris to Saint Peter's Church,
> Or I will drag thee on a hurdle thither.
> Out, you green-sickness carrion! Out, you baggage!
> You tallow-face! *(pulls his hand back as if to hit her)*

JULIET *(on her knees, almost weeping)*
> Good father, I beseech you on my knees,
> Hear me with patience but to speak a word.

CAPULET *(yelling)*
> Hang thee, young baggage! Disobedient wretch!
> I tell thee what: Get thee to church o' Thursday,
> Or never after look me in the face:
> Speak not, reply not, do not answer me;
> My fingers itch. (again makes motion as if to hit her,
> then comes downstage center)
> God's bread! It makes me mad:
> Day, night, hour, tide, time, work, play,
> Alone, in company, still my care hath been
> To have her match'd: And having now provided
> A gentleman of noble parentage,
> to have a wretched puling fool,
> answer "I'll not wed";
> Graze where you will you shall not house with me:
> For, by my soul, I'll ne'er acknowledge thee.

Exit CAPULET *stage rear.*

JULIET *(still on the floor)*
> Is there no pity sitting in the clouds,
> That sees into the bottom of my grief?
> O, sweet my mother, cast me not away!
> *(holds arms outstretched)*

LADY CAPULET *(turns completely away)*
> Talk not to me, for I'll not speak a word:
> Do as thou wilt, for I have done with thee.

Exit **LADY CAPULET** *stage rear.*

NURSE *comes up from behind* **JULIET** *and puts her arms around her, comfortingly.* **JULIET** *cries on her shoulder.*

JULIET
> O nurse, What say'st thou? Hast thou not a word of joy?
> Some comfort, nurse.

NURSE
> Faith, here it is.
> Romeo is banished and all the world to nothing
> That he dares ne'er come back to challenge you,
> Or, if he do, it needs must be by stealth.
> Then, since the case so stands as now it doth.
> I think it best you married with the County.
> O, he's a lovely gentleman!
> Romeo's a dishclout to him. An eagle, madam,
> Hath not so green, so quick, so fair an eye
> as Paris hath. Beshrew my heart,
> I think you are happy in this second match,
> For it excels your first, or, if it did not,
> your first is dead, or 'twere as good he were
> As living here and you no use of him.

JULIET *(gets up from bed, facing downstage, not looking at* **NURSE***)*
Well, thou hast comforted me marvelous much.
Go in: And tell my lady I am gone,
Having displeased my father, to Laurence' cell,
To make confession and to be absolved.

NURSE
Marry, I will; and this is wisely done.

Exit **NURSE** *stage rear.*

JULIET
I'll to the friar, to know his remedy:
If all else fail, myself have power to die.

Exit **JULIET** *stage left.*

✳ *ROMEO AND JULIET:* PERFORMANCE NOTES

I directed this production of *Romeo and Juliet* in 2005 with a ninth grade English class. It was a challenging and rewarding season for me. I had some discipline issues that year. I had the impression that my actors were pushing me, or testing me, and I yelled at them two days in a row during the rehearsal period, which backfired a bit because it took some of the fun out of the process. I later apologized for it, and we eventually got back on track and started having fun with the play again, resulting in a lively and satisfying performance from the group. That was a learning experience for me, and in subsequent years I have refrained from raising my voice in that way. It is possible that I had some growing up to do, too.

While directing Act III, Scene V, during which Lord Capulet yells at Juliet for disobeying his directive that she should marry Paris, I suggest to the actor playing Capulet that he pretend he is Mr. Newlin yelling at the class. There are times when art can indeed imitate life. Ninth graders have rich emotional lives (as do teachers), so *Romeo and Juliet* is a play they can sink their teeth into. Playing a tragedy is tricky because comedy is never very far away.

The most memorable moment in this production of *Romeo and Juliet* comes in Act V, Scene III, the final scene at the tomb. I had mentioned to the actress playing Lady Capulet that it was okay to cry at Juliet's tomb. What I was not prepared for was what she chose to do instead: She let out a piercing, high-pitched shriek, cried, "My baby!" at the top of her lungs, and slid on her knees with her arms outstretched to dead Juliet's side, to sidesplitting extended laughter from the audience. So much for tragedy. After that incident, I made it a policy to implement stern warnings about "experimenting" with alternate interpretations on show day. The experimentation should take place during the rehearsal process, not performances. When you bring yourself to a role with enthusiasm, it creates an indelible portrait of a character. If you foster an attitude of fun, and mine the text with the group for clues to what gives the character life, then anything is possible when performing Shakespeare.

Playing tragedy can be tricky. You are just as apt to laugh as to cry. Small details in how the lines are said or how bodies move can result in unintended laughter. Ultimately, I am glad when the actors commit to their performances.

The following comments are the result of reviewing a DVD of my ninth grade group's performance of *Romeo and Juliet* at the Folger Library Secondary School Shakespeare Festival. A video camera mounted on a tripod is one of the best study tools around. Watching a DVD of the rehearsal or show frequently unearths small details that are missed the first time around.

ROMEO AND JULIET: ACT III, SCENE V

Romeo and Juliet kiss in this scene (Act III, Scene V). There are some issues surrounding kissing. I had tried to get a feel for this by asking on the questionnaire if the student would be willing to kiss another student in the play (with some hilarious responses). The issue was not whether the actors were willing to kiss (they were)—the issue was the parents. Several parents were unhappy with the idea of their sons and daughters kissing on stage. (Parents apparently had no problem with theatrical depictions of murder and suicide.) We circumvented the issue by having characters turn their heads and kiss on the cheek, while making it look like they were kissing on the lips. In the heat of the performance, the actors basically made their own decisions, and it looked real enough to me!

Little gestures in this dramatic scene can go a long way toward painting a visual picture of the relationships between characters. Upon entering and seeing Juliet weeping, Lady Capulet can reach out her hand to hold Juliet's hand. Similar choices can be made in Juliet's exchanges with the Nurse and Lord Capulet. Experiment with different potential responses by Juliet to see which resonates most with you and the actors. Juliet can pull her hand away. Juliet can hold her mother's hand but not maintain eye contact. Juliet can cry into her mother's arms. Each moment in a scene offers the actor and director a choice on how to speak the lines, which words to stress, and how to physicalize the interchange. Experiment with the options to give yourself a rich palette from which to paint the picture of the play.

At the Folger Library Secondary School Shakespeare Festival, students only perform the play once. There are no second chances. If you are fortunate enough to be able to mount the performance for several shows, then what goes awry in the first performance can be fixed for the second. Use a video camera to capture all the details that you might miss, and then look for positive aspects of the your work while also finding ways you might improve your performance.

✳ ROMEO AND JULIET: MONOLOGUE NOTES

ACT III, SCENE V: NURSE MONOLOGUE

Nurse has a special and intimate relationship with Juliet as she has known her since she was born. Nurse is Juliet's ally and confidante and has gone so far as to seek Romeo out in public to deliver Juliet's invitation to him. Yet in this scene, on the heels of Romeo's banishment, when Juliet begs Nurse for some words of comfort, Nurse now insists that Juliet will be better off marrying Paris.

This is a poignant piece that represents a turning point in the lifelong relationship between Nurse and Juliet: Nurse is no longer able to support or encourage Juliet's heart's desire. As a result, she loses Juliet's trust and ultimately Juliet herself.

As with all pieces of theatre, you have choices to make as an actor regarding emotional attitude, vocal tone, word emphasis, physical movement, and facial expression. You will choose an interpretation for each moment. Is Nurse facing Juliet? Is she standing behind her? Is she avoiding eye contact with Juliet and performing a chore such as making the bed?

If playing the scene with Juliet, Nurse will of course react to Juliet herself on the stage. If the scene is played as a solo monologue, Nurse should react to "Juliet" at a chosen point in the passage and decide what Juliet is doing or not doing with her face and body. You can then determine how this affects Nurse emotionally.

Does the tone shift at any point during the monologue? After Nurse exclaims, "I think it best you married with the County," there might be a change in Nurse's attitude and demeanor, as if after stating this opinion, she now has to back it up with supporting facts to bolster her case.

Thus, phrases describing Paris's virtues—"lovely gentleman," "an eagle, madam," and "so fair an eye"—can be spoken with vigor and conviction, whereas words to describe Romeo, such as the classic "dishclout," can be tossed off with a mock disgust.

There could be an increase in Nurse's conviction and overall intensity with the phrase "Beshrew my heart, I think you are happy in this second match." Implicit here is that Nurse is trying to convince herself as much as Juliet. What is the subtext? Does Nurse truly believe that Juliet will be happier with Paris or does she know that this is the only practical choice?

Nurse can emphasize the word "dead," describing Romeo's uselessness to Juliet, and punch up the phrase "no use to him" to bring her point home. When performing any monologue, you must decide which words and phrases to emphasize and how to color them emotionally. This passage also contains rhythmic variations. Some of the lines are written in iambic pentameter, while others are not. Decide how to use these rhythmic changes to your advantage to present a dynamic monologue.

Once you have made certain choices related to how you would like to play the monologue, experiment with changing the attitude or delivery to see if this yields new insights into the text. If Nurse has been playing the lines as cheery and optimistic in an attempt to lift Juliet's spirits, you might try the lines again as more harshly realistic and didactic. The performance might have elements of both choices. For example, upon observing Juliet's horrified reaction to the suggestion that she marry Paris, the line "O, he's a lovely gentleman!" could be spoken with a forced cheeriness. "Your first is dead, or 'twere as good he were" might well resonate with resignation. Ultimately, the answers to many of our acting and interpretation questions reside in the text itself.

Familiarize yourself with the characters' lines in other scenes to round out your understanding of a role. The more you are aware of the words your character speaks throughout the entire play, the more you will understand how to deliver the lines in your particular scene or monologue.

There is a notable coda to this monologue, an interchange between Nurse and Juliet:

JULIET
> Speak'st thou from thy heart.

NURSE
> And from my soul too, else beshrew them both.

JULIET
> Amen

NURSE
> What?

The implication in this exchange is that Juliet does not believe Nurse to be speaking honestly, and Nurse realizes it. This is one reason the scene is so painful. During the monologue, Juliet's reactions affect Nurse emotionally. By the end of the scene, Juliet could be treating Nurse as coldly as a stranger, which hurts.

SUGGESTED VIEWING

ROMEO AND JULIET, 1936
Director: George Cukor
Starring: Leslie Howard, Norma Shearer

ROMEO AND JULIET, 1968
Director: Franco Zeffirelli
Starring: Leonard Whiting, Olivia Hussey

✴ THE TAMING OF THE SHREW

CHARACTERS IN THE PLAY

The following is a list of characters that appear in this scene of The Taming of the Shrew.

KATHERINE: Baptista's elder daughter, sister to Bianca
BIANCA: Baptista's younger daughter, sister to Katherine
PETRUCHIO: Suitor to Katherine
BAPTISTA: Father to Katherine and Bianca
LUCENTIO: Suitor to Bianca
BIONDELLO: Servant to Lucentio
HORTENSIO: Suitor to Bianca
GREMIO: Suitor to Bianca
WIDOW
GRUMIO: Servant to Petruchio
CHORUS
NARRATOR

SET AND PROP LIST

SET PIECES:
Stool
Four benches

PROPS:
Pillows and sheets for bed

✳ *THE TAMING OF THE SHREW:*
ACT V, SCENE II

Padua, the home of Lucentio.

CHORUS *stands and dances around the stage, chanting,* "The party, the party, of Petruchio and Katherina."

ALL *form a semicircle upstage center, facing audience. There are three couples:* LUCENTIO *and* BIANCA *in the middle,* PETRUCHIO *and* KATHERINE *on the right, and* HORTENSIO *and* WIDOW *on the left.* BAPTISTA *stands to the right of* PETRUCHIO.

LUCENTIO
> At last, though long, our jarring notes agree
> And time it is when raging war is done
> To smile at 'scapes and perils overblown.
> My fair Bianca, bid my father welcome,
> While I with selfsame kindness welcome thine.
> Brother Petruchio, sister Katherina,
> And thou, Hortensio, with thy loving widow,
> Feast with the best, and welcome to my house.

BAPTISTA
> Now, in good sadness, son Petruchio,
> I think thou hast the veriest shrew of all.

Exit BIANCA, KATHERINE, *and* WIDOW *to the downstage right corner of the stage, insulted by that comment.*

PETRUCHIO
> Well, I say no. And therefore, for assurance,
> Let's each one send unto his wife,
> And he whose wife is most obedient
> To come at first when he doth send for her
> Shall win the wager which we will propose.

HORTENSIO
> Content, what's the wager?

LUCENTIO
> A hundred crowns.

HORTENSIO
> Content.

PETRUCHIO
> A match! 'Tis done.

LUCENTIO *(to* BIONDELLO*)*
> Go, Biondello, bid your mistress come to me.

BIONDELLO
> I go.

Exit BIONDELLO *quickly downstage right to query* BIANCA.
BIONDELLO *appears to be asking* BIANCA *a question, and she shakes her head "no."*

Re-enter BIONDELLO *immediately.*

LUCENTIO
> How now, what news?

BIONDELLO *(to* LUCENTIO*)*
> Sir, my mistress sends you word
> That she is busy, and she cannot come.

LUCENTIO *appears shocked, embarrassed, and dismayed.*

ALL *laugh, mocking him.*

PETRUCHIO *(laughing, mocking)*
> How? "She's busy, and she cannot come"?
> Is that an answer?

GREMIO
> Ay, and a kind one, too.
> Pray God, sir, your wife send you not a worse.

HORTENSIO
> Sirrah Biondello, go and entreat my wife
> To come to me forthwith.

Exit BIONDELLO *quickly to* WIDOW *downstage right with other women.* WIDOW *also shakes her head "no."*

Re-enter BIONDELLO.

HORTENSIO *(haltingly, stuttering)*
> Now, where's my wife?

BIONDELLO
> She says you have some goodly jest in hand.
> She will not come. She bids you come to her.

ALL *laugh, mocking* HORTENSIO, *who is embarrassed and flustered.*

PETRUCHIO *(amused)*
> Worse and worse. She will not come!
> O vile, intolerable, not to be endured!

    Sirrah Grumio, go to your mistress,
    Say I command her come to me.

Exit GRUMIO *toward the women downstage right.*

Enter KATHERINE *with* BIANCA *and* WIDOW *from downstage right.*

KATHERINE
    What is your will, sir, that you send for me?

BAPTISTA
    Now fair befall thee, good Petruchio!
    For she is changed as she had never been.

PETRUCHIO
    Nay, I will show more sign of her obedience,
    Her new built virtue and obedience.
    Katherine, that cap of yours becomes you not.
    Off with that bauble, throw it underfoot.

KATHERINE *obeys and throws the cap under her own foot, grinding it into the ground.*

BIANCA
    Fie, what a foolish duty call you this?

LUCENTIO
    I would your duty were as foolish too.
    The wisdom of your duty, fair Bianca,
    Hath cost me a hundred crowns since suppertime.

BIANCA
    The more fool you for laying on my duty.

PETRUCHIO

Katherine, I charge thee tell these headstrong women
What duty they do owe their lords and husbands.

WIDOW

Come, come. You're mocking. We will have no telling.

KATHERINE

Fie, fie! Unknit that threat'ning unkind brow,
And dart not scornful glances from those eyes
To wound thy lord, thy king, thy governor.
It blots thy beauty as frosts do bite the meads,
Confounds thy fame as whirlwinds shake fair buds,
And in no sense is meet or amiable.
A woman moved is like a fountain troubled,
Muddy, ill-seeming, thick, bereft of beauty,
And while it is so, none so dry or thirsty
Will deign to sip or touch one drop of it.
Thy husband is thy lord, thy life, thy keeper,
Thy head, thy sovereign, one that cares for thee,
And for thy maintenance commits his body
To painful labor both by sea and land,
To watch the night in storms, the day in cold,
Whilst thou liest warm at home, secure and safe,
And craves no other tribute at thy hands
But love, fair looks, and true obedience—
Too little payment for so great a debt.
Such duty as the subject owes the prince,
Even such a woman oweth to her husband;
And when she is froward, peevish, sullen, sour,
And not obedient to his honest will,
What is she but a foul contending rebel
And graceless traitor to her loving lord?
I am ashamed that women are so simple
To offer war where they should kneel for peace,
Or seek for rule, supremacy, and sway

When they are bound to serve, love, and obey.
Why are our bodies soft and weak and smooth,
Unapt to toil and trouble in the world,
But that our soft conditions and our hearts
Should well agree with our external parts?
Come, come, you froward and unable worms!
My mind hath been as big as one of yours,
My heart as great, my reason haply more,
To bandy word for word and frown for frown;
But now I see our lances are but straws,
Our strength as weak, our weakness past compare,
That seeming to be most which we indeed least are.
Then vail your stomachs, for it is no boot,
And place your hands below your husband's foot;
In token of which duty, if he please,
My hand is ready, may it do him ease.

KATHERINE *puts her hand down on the ground, and* PETRUCHIO
puts his foot gently on it.

PETRUCHIO
> Why, there's a wench! Come on, and kiss me, Kate.

KATHERINE *and* PETRUCHIO *kiss.*

ALL *stand and form a circle facing outward.*

(FROM INDUCTION, SCENE II)

ALL
> We all have come to play a pleasant comedy
> Seeing too much sadness hath congealed your blood,
> Therefore we thought it good you hear a play
> Which bars a thousand harms and lengthens life!

ALL *hold hands and take a bow. Exeunt.*

✳ *THE TAMING OF THE SHREW:* PERFORMANCE NOTES

When I staged this 2008 production of *The Taming of the Shrew,* it was my eighteenth consecutive year of conducting a teaching-artist residency in the D.C. public schools system, under the auspices of the Folger Shakespeare Library, and my first time staging a show in the round. This was not by choice. The Folger professional acting company was staging *Richard III* in the round, and performers at the Secondary School Shakespeare Festival at the Folger must stage their play on whatever set the Folger acting company is using at their Elizabethan theater.

In our production, all actors stayed on stage throughout the performance, which was also a first for me. The students were seated on benches, four actors to a bench, with a total of sixteen cast members. During their scenes, the actors simply stood up from their benches and performed in the playing area between the benches rather than entering from the wings.

When not up on their feet acting, the remaining cast members served as the Chorus, providing a vocal and physical group response to the action on the stage. This made for a lively and fast-paced production with full participation and a commedia dell'arte feel, which fit the setting of the village of Padua and the raucous mood of the play.

For the purposes of this cutting, I adjusted the placement of the benches to reflect proscenium seating. For the staging in this text, I placed two benches upstage right and two benches upstage left, with four actors on each bench. Should you wish to adjust the staging to include more entrances and exits from offstage, the script is easily adapted to conventional staging, and you can still keep the Chorus participation intact for times when more actors are on stage. I will say that for this play, having the acting company onstage for the whole show gave the production a momentum and zest that would have been diluted with more conventional staging.

I did encounter some sight line issues with my blocking, however. Because the play was in the round, when the Chorus stood on the sidelines, they impeded the view of the characters in the middle of the stage. A performance of this version of *The Taming of the Shrew* on a conventional proscenium stage will not have the same issues. If I ever stage something in the round again, I will be more aware of this visibility issue and space my actors farther apart during crowd scenes, moving them closer to the "corners" of the playing area.

The Taming of the Shrew is a merry, madcap romp, and one that young actors relish. It is a challenge to stage due to the sheer physicality of the Kate-Petruchio interchanges. We worked slowly and methodically, taking great care to make sure all the "fight" scenes were safe. Ultimately, it was a great group effort and a spirited time featuring one of Shakespeare's best-matched pair of warriors in the battle of the sexes: Petruchio and Kate.

Our 2014 performance began with a merry Italian accordion tune played on a small portable stereo. The stereo initially malfunctioned, leaving a confused and scrambling cast offstage, waiting for the sound issue to be resolved. Next time, I will address the possibility of technical difficulties and instruct the actors to ignore malfunctioning equipment and simply enter with energy! It is more important for the performance to get underway than for a sound cue to work, but actors need to have these contingencies spelled out for them ahead of time. As a bumper sticker of mine says: "Plan to improvise."

Although we only use a drum, a recorder, and a siren for our subsequent sound effects, the timing of each sound greatly enhances the theatricality of our raucous entrance—and unlike the stereo, these instruments do not require batteries. When given a choice between pre-recorded music and live music played by cast members, always choose live music. The actor who played the recorder had to learn basic fingering and blowing. I provided her with some instruction, but if you do not know how to play the instrument in question, YouTube is an endlessly helpful source of free tutorials.

The actress playing Katherine in this first scene was a spirited force: She grabbed Gremio's cane from him and waved it over his head threateningly as he hung onto Baptista to avoid falling down. There was nothing artificial-looking about it. When one actor in a play or scene commits fully, the other actors rise to the same level of commitment.

Numerous running gags involving the Chorus recur throughout the first two scenes. The Chorus cheers and raises their arms in the air ("Hey!") each time the word "Padua" is uttered. They also coo "Aww" whenever Bianca's name is mentioned, which causes Bianca to stand from her chair and curtsy, acknowledging the applause. These repeated sound effects establish the Chorus as a character in the play.

We opened Act I, Scene II with a silent vignette. Petruchio and Grumio come to Padua, steal some flowers from a flower vendor, and present them to a pair of village ladies. This is a short bit, but it establishes Petruchio as a rogue and Grumio as his sidekick. When Petruchio knocks on Lucentio's door, all Chorus members stomp their feet on the floor to create a "knocking" sound. This type of group sound effect takes some practice and concentration, but the effect of a unified Chorus is powerful and worth the effort to achieve.

Actors in a Shakespearean production must have an understanding of text and subtext and the ability to share that with the audience. The study and performance of Shakespeare always starts with the words themselves. Enjoy the way the words feel tripping off your tongue. Shakespeare's words are fun to speak.

Petruchio's speaking the name "Kate" can be an opportunity for the actor playing Petruchio to experiment with different ways of saying her name: sweetly, curtly, mockingly, softly, or in a sing-song style. Each time he says her name, Petruchio can come right up to Kate's ear, pause, and then speak the name.

In our production, we played Act II, Scene I as a boxing match with Chorus as cheering spectators. Katherine appears to concede to Petruchio's "Kiss me Kate" command and allows him into her arms. She then stomps on his foot, which is accompanied by a Chorus member making a squeaky sound with a clown horn. That's comedy!

We found a commedia dell'arte mask for Litio (Hortensio in disguise) to wear. If you plan to introduce a mask, beard, or other potentially cumbersome prop or costume piece into a production, do so as early in the rehearsal process as possible. I introduced this mask a little late, and the actress spent a significant amount of time onstage trying to keep it from falling off. Nonetheless, it was a nice touch, and a nod to the commedia dell'arte style that we brought to the production.

The wedding scene began with a chanting dance around the stage, complete with tambourines, drums, and hand claps: "The wedding, the wedding, of Petruchio and Katharina." During our performance, the audience clapped along joyously. The Chorus repeated the chant upon exiting the stage and returned a few seconds later, chanting, "They're married!" Repetition enhances comedy, especially when one employs the rule of three: 1) start a theme, 2) establish the theme by repeating it, and 3) break the theme by inserting an unexpected change. Adding to the comedy was the ridiculously short 30-second interval between the group's leaving the stage for the wedding and returning after it. Comedy can be absurd; conventional rules of time and space do not have to apply.

The actress playing Katherine in this scene chose to portray a genuinely despondent and heartbroken bride left at the altar. She cried and threw her flowers to the ground before slumping in her seat. Just because it is a comedy does not mean the emotions are not real. In fact, playing a character's negative feelings earnestly often serves a comedy better than mugging or creating a caricature of an emotion.

THE TAMING OF THE SHREW: ACT V, SCENE II

The Chorus had an exceptionally good time making fun of Lucentio and Hortensio during this scene as they bid their wives to come and their wives refuse. Upon seeing Biondello return alone, the actor playing Hortensio gave out a plaintive stutter: "N...n...now, where's my wife?" That small comic adjustment paid off in a big laugh. This was a stutter of the actor's choosing.

Katherine's final speech is problematic for modern audiences. How are we to reconcile the line, "Thy husband is thy lord, thy life, thy keeper, thy head, thy sovereign" with the proud and wild Katherine of earlier in the play? The challenge is up to the actor to find something in the words that makes sense to her.

I encouraged the actor playing Katherine in this scene to study the speech and see if there were any words or phrases that she could apply to an aspect of her own life or her relationships. I shared with the class a few of my own personal interpretations based upon my own relationships, not just with my spouse but with other entities, some of them perhaps not human (e.g., God or Spirit). One beauty of Shakespeare's language is that it is poetic and opens itself up to interpretation on a number of levels. The words do not have to be taken literally; they might be interpreted metaphorically, ironically, humorously, or bitterly.

Ultimately, the student playing Katherine made her own choices, having studied other actors' versions of the speech on film, and thought about what the words meant to her personally. I believe our entire acting company as well as the audience left the theater with our own personal interpretation of *The Taming of the Shrew.* We also all left the theater with at least one experience in common: We laughed!

✳ THE TAMING OF THE SHREW: MONOLOGUE NOTES

ACT V, SCENE II: KATHERINE MONOLOGUE

This is a tricky monologue to interpret. Katherine has exhibited a dramatic turnaround from a headstrong and imposingly independent figure to a wife who will kneel at her husband's feet on command. There are two fundamentally opposing possibilities on how to play this speech: 1) Katherine has changed and believes every word she says about wives' duties to husbands or 2) Katherine is delivering the speech ironically and is still the same belligerent person; she is simply acting. I have seen versions of the play using the latter approach where Katherine winks at the end to fully indicate that she does not believe what she says.

Either approach is valid, and of course there are ways of playing the words so that Katherine may speak some parts of the speech earnestly and others ironically. The best film version I have found of this play is the 1967 classic directed by Franco Zeffirelli, which stars Elizabeth Taylor as Katherine and Richard Burton as Petruchio. What impresses me about Taylor's rendering of the final speech is that she keeps Katherine's intensity and "spit and vinegar" when she speaks to the ladies (specifically Bianca and Widow but also the other women at the party) but softens her tone with Petruchio, even displaying genuine love for him.

There are two other noteworthy film versions: the 1976 version staged in commedia dell'arte style by the American Conservatory Theater in San Francisco (distributed by the Broadway Theatre

Archive/kultur.com) and the 1929 film with Mary Pickford as Katherine and Douglas Fairbanks as Petruchio. In both of these versions, Katherine winks at the end of her speech to indicate that she does not really believe her own words.

Elizabeth Taylor's version works for me because it is believable and has an emotional impact. It is plausible because Katherine's essential toughness remains. She barks her criticisms to the women in a shrill tone, spitting the words out with the same fervor that she does throughout the play in her battles with Petruchio. When she speaks with Petruchio, though, her tonality softens considerably, and aided by swelling music, she becomes visibly emotional. Her eyes well up, and her voice takes on a soft and loving timbre as if she is smitten with Petruchio.

One reason I favor this approach from a dramatic point of view is that it allows for dynamics. By retaining her shrewish tone and body language while chastising the women and mitigating that harshness in her words to Petruchio, the audience experiences a Kate whose heated opinions still burn with the fire we have grown to know and love. At the same time, she has developed a warmer, gentler approach with Petruchio, whom she may be coming to love or simply learning to control through modifying her behavior. The end result is the same from a theatrical standpoint: Katherine is no longer a one-dimensional character and is therefore more compelling.

Try the monologue with this approach: harsh with the women and more sweet-tempered with Petruchio. See if the words match the demeanor. Using this tactic, the first ten lines of the speech—"Fie, fie!" through "one drop of it"—address the women. Imbue the words "threatening," "unkind," "scornful," and "blots" with a tone of disdain. Perhaps on the four descriptive terms ("muddy," "ill-seeming," "thick," and "bereft of beauty"), you could turn your regard to a different woman with each word or phrase, as if singling out individual ladies.

The next set of eleven lines, starting with "Thy husband" and ending again with the word "husband," can be addressed endearingly to Petruchio. Notice the words here: "lord," "life" "keeper", "head", and "sovereign." They are strong words, signifying devotion. The notes to the Folger Shakespeare Library edition of *The Taming of the Shrew* refer to "Paul's letter to Ephesians 5:22: 'Husband is head of the wife even as Christ is head of the church.'" This was the prevalent Christian view of marriage: The wife is obedient to the husband.

The biblical references may reinforce the idea of dedication to a power greater than us. It is difficult in the twenty-first century for many of us to conceive of the husband as lord to the wife. This seems an outdated notion in our culture today. But the idea of religious faithfulness, or devotion to something greater than ourselves, is a constant through time and across cultures. Thinking of Katherine's newfound loyalty to Petruchio in terms of other allegiances—to a deity, a royal figure, a higher power, or a higher ideal—may facilitate your interpretation of this monologue as an actor.

There is another interesting acting and staging choice to watch for in the 1967 Taylor/Burton film. When Katherine exclaims, "Then vail your stomachs, for it is no boot,/And place your hands below your husband's foot," she pushes the two ladies on either side of her to their knees. Again, the aggressive, hot-headed side of Katherine remains in full force in her admonition to her fellow women.

For her final two lines in this film version, Katherine softens again and kneels herself. She coos, "In token of which duty, if he please/My hand is ready, may it do him ease." She stretches out the word "ease" so that it floats gently in the air, finishing the speech on a soft and conciliatory note.

I am not suggesting that you base your monologue and staging choices exclusively on this film. Elizabeth Taylor's interpretation of Katherine impressed me because of the powerful acting decisions that she made. I urge you to make your own strong choices for the character of Katherine. They can be inspired by other versions that you have seen, but ultimately the best choices for your performance will be uniquely your own.

In fact, with any monologue, I urge you to start with the text and the words themselves. Study their meaning in literal, historical/ religious, and metaphorical terms. Make sure that you have read and understood the entire play, taking note of the characters' relationships, words, and dramatic arcs from beginning to end. The monologue does not exist in a vacuum. It is part of the individual's journey from the opening scene to the curtain call.

Katherine has gone on a unique dramatic voyage in *The Taming of the Shrew*, and she has apparently changed. If you play this transformation from a fiercely fighting independent woman to a devoted wife as genuine rather than ironic, it may have a greater emotional impact on your audience. On the other hand, it may also be harder to convince the audience of Katherine's sincerity in her devotion, given her combative history. But it is well worth the challenge.

As an actor, the choice is always yours as to how you will interpret Shakespeare's words. You are putting much of yourself into the character. The human qualities of Katherine can exist on the page, but they do not come to life without a performer to provide the living, breathing, fighting, crying, laughing, loving vessel for all of Katherine's deep complexity. Enjoy portraying this indelible Shakespearean character: one of theatre's most memorable individualists.

SUGGESTED VIEWING

THE TAMING OF THE SHREW, 1967
Director: Franco Zeffirelli
Starring: Elizabeth Taylor, Richard Burton

THE TAMING OF THE SHREW, 1976
Directors: William Ball, Kirk Browning
Starring: Fredi Olster, Marc Singer

✴ THE TEMPEST

CHARACTERS IN THE PLAY

The following is a list of characters that appear in this scene of The Tempest.

PROSPERO: Former Duke of Milan, now a magician on a
   Mediterranean island

ARIEL: An airy spirit, servant to Prospero

ALONSO: King of Naples

GONZALO: Counselor to Alonso, and friend to Prospero

SEBASTIAN: Alonso's brother

ANTONIO: Usurping Duke of Milan, and Prospero's brother

FERDINAND: Prince of Naples, and Alonso's son

MIRANDA: Prospero's daughter

MASTER OF THE SHIP

BOATSWAIN OF THE SHIP

CALIBAN: A savage inhabitant of the island, servant to Prospero

STEPHANO: Alonso's drunken butler

TRINCULO: Servant to Alonso

NARRATOR

SET AND PROP LIST

SET PIECES:
Two stools
Chair

PROPS:
Cape or cloak, staff for Prospero

✳ *THE TEMPEST:* ACT V, SCENE I

Before Prospero's cell.

Enter NARRATOR *from stage rear, coming downstage center.*

NARRATOR
> Prospero releases Alonso and his party from their
> charmed state and renounces the further use of
> his magic. Prospero's dukedom is restored, all is
> forgiven, and family members are reunited. Almost
> everyone is well on the way to being free! This must
> be a Shakespearean comedy!

Exit NARRATOR *stage left.*

Enter PROSPERO, *in his magician's robes, and* ARIEL *from
stage right.*

PROSPERO
> Now does my project gather to a head:
> My charms crack not; my spirits obey.
> How fares the king and his followers?

ARIEL
> Just as you left them; all prisoners, sir,
> Gonzalo's tears run down his beard, like winter's
> > drops
> From eaves of reeds.

PROSPERO *(to* **ARIEL***)*

> Hast thou, which art but air, a touch, a feeling
> Of their afflictions, and shall not myself,
> One of their kind, that relish all as sharply
> Passion as they, be kindlier moved than thou art?
> Though with their high wrongs I am struck to th' quick,
> Yet with my nobler reason 'gainst my fury
> Do I take part. The rarer action is
> In virtue than in vengeance. They being penitent,
> The sole drift of my purpose doth extend
> Not a frown further. Go, release them, Ariel.
> My charms I'll break, their senses I'll restore,
> And they shall be themselves.
> I have bedimmed
> The noontide sun, called forth the mutinous winds,
> And 'twixt the green sea and the azured vault
> Set roaring war; to the dread rattling thunder
> Have I given fire, and rifted Jove's stout oak
> With his own bolt.
> But this rough magic
> I here abjure, and when I have required
> Some heavenly music, which even now I do,

PROSPERO *gestures with his staff.*

> To work mine end upon their senses that
> This airy charm is for, I'll break my staff,
> Bury it certain fathoms in the earth,
> And deeper than did ever plummet sound
> I'll drown my book.

SOUND OPERATOR *plays* Sound Cue #1 ("Hypnotic music").

Re-enter **ARIEL** *from stage right.* **ALONSO** *follows, attended by* **GONZALO**, **SEBASTIAN**, *and* **ANTONIO**. *As* **PROSPERO** *"conducts" their movements,* **ALL** *walk around the stage in a circle, ending*

*by forming a semicircle that faces the audience. They
stand, charmed.*

SOUND OPERATOR *plays* Sound Cue #2 ("Ding").

ALL *unfreeze.*

> There stand,
> For you are spell-stopp'd.
> Most cruelly didst thou, Alonso, use me and my
> daughter:
> Thy brother was a furtherer in the act,
> Would here have kill'd your king;
> Quickly, spirit; thou shalt ere long be free.

ARIEL *(singing)*
> Merrily, merrily shall I live now
> Under the blossom that hangs on the bough.

PROSPERO
> My dainty Ariel! To the king's ship,
> There shalt thou find the master and the boatswain.
> Enforce them to this place, presently.

ARIEL
> I drink the air before me, and return.

SOUND OPERATOR *plays* Sound Cue #3 ("Ding").

Exit **ARIEL** *stage left.*

PROSPERO *(to* **ALONSO***)*
> Behold, sir king,
> The wronged Duke of Milan, Prospero.

ALONSO
> Thy pulse
> Beats as of flesh and blood; and, since I saw thee,
> The affliction of my mind amends,
> Thy dukedom I resign and do entreat
> Thou pardon me my wrongs.

PROSPERO *(aside to* SEBASTIAN *and* ANTONIO*)*
> But you, my brace of lords, were I so minded,
> I here could justify you traitors.

SEBASTIAN *(aside)*
> The devil speaks in him.

PROSPERO *(to* ANTONIO*)*
> No. For you, most wicked sir, I do forgive
> Thy rankest fault.

ALONSO
> I have lost my dear son Ferdinand.

PROSPERO
> I have lost my daughter.
> I will requite you with as good a thing.

Enter FERDINAND *and* MIRANDA *from stage left.* ALONSO *is astonished and joyful to see his son alive.*

ALONSO
> If this prove
> A vision of the Island, one dear son
> Shall I twice lose.

SEBASTIAN
> A most high miracle!

FERDINAND *(to* ALONSO*)*

    Though the seas threaten, they are merciful;
    I have cursed them without cause. (kneels)

MIRANDA *(looking at men with amazement and attraction)*

    O, wonder!
    How many goodly creatures are there here!
    How beauteous mankind is! O brave new world,
    That has such people in't!

PROSPERO

    'Tis new to thee.

ALONSO

    Is she the goddess that hath sever'd us,
    And brought us thus together?

FERDINAND

    Sir, she is mortal;
    But by immortal Providence she's mine:
    She is daughter to this famous Duke of Milan,
    And second father this lady makes him to me.

ALONSO

    I am hers:
    (to MIRANDA*)* I must ask my child forgiveness!
    (to FERDINAND *and* MIRANDA*)* Give me your hands.

GONZALO

    Be it so! Amen!

Re-enter ARIEL *from stage left, with* MASTER *and* BOATSWAIN *following in amazement.*

    What is the news?

240 * THE 30-MINUTE SHAKESPEARE ANTHOLOGY

BOATSWAIN
We have safely found
Our king and company. Our ship—
Which we gave out split—
Is tight and yare and bravely rigg'd as when
We first put out to sea.

PROSPERO *(aside to* ARIEL*)*
My tricksy spirit!
Thou shalt be free.
Set Caliban and his companions free;
Untie the spell.

Exit ARIEL *stage left.*

PROSPERO *(to* ALONSO*)*
How fares my gracious sir?
There are yet missing of your company.

Re-enter ARIEL *from stage left, driving in* CALIBAN, STEPHANO, *and* TRINCULO.

SEBASTIAN
Ha, ha!
What things are these, my lord Antonio?
Will money buy 'em?

ANTONIO
One of them
Is a plain fish, and, no doubt, marketable.

PROSPERO
This misshapen demi-devil
had plotted with them to take my life.

CALIBAN
> I shall be pinch'd to death.

ALONSO
> Is not this Stephano, my drunken butler?
> And Trinculo is reeling ripe:
> How camest thou in this pickle?

TRINCULO
> I have been in such a pickle since I
> saw you last.

SEBASTIAN
> How now, Stephano!

STEPHANO
> I am not Stephano, but a cramp.

PROSPERO *(pointing to* CALIBAN*)*
> Go, sirrah, to my cell.

CALIBAN
> Ay, that I will; what a thrice-double ass
> Was I, to take this drunkard for a god
> And worship this dull fool!

Exit CALIBAN, STEPHANO, *and* TRINCULO *stage left.*

PROSPERO
> Your highness; in the morn
> I'll bring you to your ship;
> And thence retire me to my Milan, where
> Every third thought shall be my grave.

ALONSO

> I long
> To hear the story of your life, which must
> Take the ear strangely.

PROSPERO

> I'll deliver all;
> And promise you calm seas, auspicious gales.
> *(aside to* ARIEL*)* My Ariel, chick,
> To the elements be free, and fare thou well!

Exit ARIEL *stage left.*

PROSPERO

> Now my charms are all o'erthrown,
> And what strength I have's mine own,
> But release me from my bands
> With the help of your good hands:
> As you from crimes would pardon'd be,
> Let your indulgence set me free.

Re-enter ALL *from stage left.*

ALL

> Our revels now are ended. These our actors,
> Were all spirits and
> Are melted into air, into thin air:
> We are such stuff
> As dreams are made on, and our little life
> Is rounded with a sleep.

ALL *hold hands and take a bow. Exeunt.*

✳ *THE TEMPEST:* PERFORMANCE NOTES

I directed this version of *The Tempest* in 2011 with a group of high school seniors. The play is ideal for novice actors and allows them to enter a fantastic new world full of colorful characters and beguiling language.

Simple sound effects played live contribute to the air of magic in this play. When Prospero waves his hand to put Miranda to sleep, the sound operator strikes a "ding" on the triangle, and as Ariel enters for the first time, she plays the recorder. For my 2011 production, I gave a basic recorder instruction to the actresses cast in the role. Likewise with drums and triangle, I imparted my musical knowledge to the cast, many of whom had never played these instruments. If you do not have musical ability or experience yourself, you can take a brief lesson in the instruments used in the play, or seek out a YouTube video on the subject. Local music stores can refer you to a good teacher if you are feeling adventurous.

One actress who played Ariel skipped and spun around while she walked, her eyes twinkling with the magic of her character. In later scenes, another student portrayed Ariel. When you have two actors splitting a role, encourage them to watch each other play the part and, if possible, find a common theatrical vocabulary: physical mannerisms or vocal inflections that identify the character.

This will make it easier for the audience to understand the transition, and reinforce to the actors that a person's uniqueness can be depicted using specific techniques. (For example, consider how a character stands or walks and then try to illustrate that physically.) Emphasize that the text is the first and best place to look for clues about a role. Investigate not only what the characters say, but also what other characters say about them.

Ariel uses scarves to accent her movements, holding one in each hand and swinging them about herself gracefully. Often the simplest of props and costume pieces add much to a character's look and overall dramatic impression. Prospero has a staff that he uses both to lean on, contributing to his appearance as an old man, and as a magic wand. Perhaps his years fall away when he uses his magic, allowing him to wave the staff with a youthful vigor, but when he is back to his more mortal self, the years return and he is older again. Props are tools by which an actor reveals elements of his character. How we interact with the physical world speaks volumes about who we are.

Every prop, set piece, and costume piece gives actors an opportunity to reveal to the audience more about themselves. Ariel, Prospero, Caliban, Miranda, and the Boatswain will all sit on a stool in a different way. For an interesting rehearsal exercise, place a stool on the stage and have your players enter and sit down one by one, using the gait and physical demeanor of their characters. By discussing the differences in each character's "sitting style," you can yield interesting insights into his or her unique personality.

We humans each have a distinct spark in us, and when an actor chooses to share that light by adding a bit of spirit to a piece of text, magic happens. Each individual contributes something special to the production that only she possesses. A great piece of art is not just technique and talent—it is spirit as well.

Actors can experiment with status by first playing the scene with one character as "high status" and then doing the same with another, taking note of what the difference yields. Either character can be played as "low status" as well, yielding four possible sets of results. Any moment in the text can be reinterpreted using simple theater techniques, which often yield fascinating revelations on how to play the interactions and the scenes themselves.

I am always excited when actors inject spark into tiny parts or seemingly minor lines. In the introduction to this scene, the narrator explains that Caliban has urged Stephano to kill Prospero, exclaiming, "What a monstrous thing to do!" As the narrator in our production recited this line, she held up her hands like claws and growled the word "monstrous" in a delightfully guttural roar. She then finished with a shiver, as if terrified herself at this prospect. As this actress adeptly demonstrated, there are no small roles.

THE TEMPEST: ACT V, SCENE I

The narrator for this scene once again seized an opportunity for a laugh by pausing between the words "This must be" and "a Shakespearean comedy" to offer her own whimsical hand gesture. Her eyes lit up and she smiled brightly, bringing the audience into her joy. Approach the play with a spirit of originality and merriment.

As with many of the Bard's plays, the conclusion of *The Tempest* becomes a bit crowded with actors. The simplest solution is often the best: Performers should form a semicircle across the stage to ensure greatest visibility. If one character is at odds with the group, she can stand off to one side to indicate the schism. Here, Caliban can separate himself from Stephano, realizing that he has been worshiping a "dull fool." During the final scene of a Shakespearean comedy, couples should unite so the audience can see their relationships come together. In this case, Miranda and Ferdinand join hands as Alonso stands on Ferdinand's other side, hand on his shoulder.

This bittersweet and fantastical comedy comes to a close with the entire group reciting the line, "We are such stuff as dreams are made of, and our little life is rounded with a sleep." Actors should inject a rising vocal energy into this final speech as they raise their arms in unison, follow the cue of Prospero, and bow happily, the proud young owners of a classic and enduring Shakespearean comedy.

Live theater is magical. It is the most dynamic form of entertainment available to us. There is nothing like the interchange between actors and audience, that vibrant energy that is created in the theater.

The Tempest is one of Shakespeare's most poetic, magical, and moving tales, and we are fortunate to be able to continue giving it life, especially with performers who can give it the vitality it deserves.

✳ *THE TEMPEST:* MONOLOGUE NOTES

ACT V, SCENE I: PROSPERO MONOLOGUE

Prospero's first words in this monologue are spoken to the spirit Ariel. He is remarking on how Ariel seems to feel for the plight of Alonso and his court ("brimful of sorrow and dismay"). Here, Prospero's anger and desire for revenge on those who have wronged him become counterbalanced by his own humanity, as reflected through the eyes of Ariel, who is not even human.

This struggle between emotion and reason, and between vengeance and virtue, is the crux of this dramatic passage. When playing Prospero, you can demonstrate that internal conflict by coloring the words and pairing them with physical movements and facial expressions that highlight Prospero's dilemma.

Words that emphasize emotion and humanity include "touch," "feeling," "relish," "sharply," "passion," "kindlier," and "moved." Decide which of these words to emphasize and how to deliver them so they resonate with human feeling.

Where might a gesture or physical action take place? Prospero is holding a staff, so he could strike his staff against the ground to emphasize an emotion, perhaps "on *struck* to the quick" or "'gainst my *fury.*" Let the text dictate what gestures might accompany the words. The line "though with their high wrongs I am struck to the quick" exudes emotion, whereas the phrase "yet with my nobler reason" indicates a rational approach. Perhaps Prospero touches his chest (heart) and then his head to indicate the physical home of his conflicting sentiments.

Maybe Prospero's voice rises in pitch as he reflects angrily on the wrongs he has suffered and then becomes softer and lower as he catches himself becoming overwrought, returning to a rational frame of mind. There are pauses, breathing points, or "beats" in each monologue. One such beat might occur prior to the line "The rarer action is in virtue than in vengeance."

This is the conclusion that Prospero finds through his internal struggle between reason and feeling. Reason wins. You can take a silent moment to allow Prospero's thought process to register with the audience. This will bring them into Prospero's mind and his world. Beats and pauses are very effective. Study the text, and say the words out loud until you find the right spot to stop, breathe, and allow the audience to join you in your character's internal journey.

After Prospero commands Ariel to release Alonso and his court, the monologue shifts into another phase. Here Prospero vividly describes the magic he has performed: "I have bedimmed the noontide sun." His language becomes more florid and descriptive. Prospero describes colors ("green sea" and "azured vault"), sounds ("roaring war" and "rattling thunder"), and natural phenomena ("given fire" and "rifted Jove's stout oak with his own bolt.") Here again Prospero can wave his staff in a semicircle or hold it like a god throwing a thunderbolt to illustrate his conjuring. When he requires "some heavenly music," he can point the staff heavenward. This is Prospero in his element, performing what he loves: magic. Your movements as Prosper should convey mastery and power.

Prospero decides that after he releases his captives from their charms, he will give up this "rough magic." Consider how you would feel if you had to give up something you loved, which you knew was simply not right? What is the feeling of giving up something, of losing something precious to us? Show this in your face and express it in your voice.

Maybe you have already felt that way about something. If you have any way to personalize Shakespeare's text and apply it to a situation in your own life, you will be able to bring yourself into the role in a truly human and universal way. This is what it is to be human: to have feelings, to have reason, to have conflicts between "virtue and vengeance" and between "reason and fury." There is some of Prospero in all of us. If you can bring a few of your own human conflicts into Prospero's struggle using Shakespeare's beautiful words, the audience will feel it.

The final few lines of the monologue start in the air and end up well below the surface of the earth. Upon exclaiming "This airy charm," Prospero can look up or look to Ariel. Note that the word "air" could have a double meaning, referring to either the air we breathe or a musical air. The notes included in the Folger Shakespeare Library's paperback texts are very handy for discovering these gems.

Prospero's last line contains the word "bury," a solemn word indeed. When a word has a possible alternate meaning (e.g., to bury a human vs. burying a staff), feel free to give it weight. Also, when you arrive at a phrase like "plummet sound," make sure to look up the definition to understand the meaning of, in this example, the nautical term. We must be familiar with the literal meaning of the words, the story behind the mythological references, and of course what the words mean to us personally.

The Tempest was Shakespeare's last play. See if that finality can inform the end of your speech. All of the feelings and conflicts Prospero has described in the passage reach a conclusion with the last four words: "I'll drown my book." By pausing slightly between each word, you can give the Bard's final words the weight and emotional gravity they deserve.

SUGGESTED VIEWING

THE TEMPEST, 1960
Director: George Schaefer
Starring: Maurice Evans, Richard Burton

THE TEMPEST, 2014
Director: Jeremy Herrin
Starring: Roger Allam, James Garnon

✳ TWELFTH NIGHT

CHARACTERS IN THE PLAY

The following is a list of characters that appear in this scene of Twelfth Night.

DUKE ORSINO: Duke of Illyria

VIOLA: A lady of Messaline shipwrecked on the coast of Illyria (disguised as a man)

CURIO: Gentleman serving Orsino

FESTE: Jester

DUKE ORSINO'S BAND

NARRATOR

SET AND PROP LIST

SET PIECES:
Bench
Table
Three chairs
Throne

PROPS:
Musical instruments for Orsino's band
Tray of fruit for Curio

✳ *TWELFTH NIGHT:* ACT II, SCENE IV

Duke Orsino's palace.

Enter **NARRATOR** *from stage rear, coming downstage center.*

NARRATOR

> Back at Duke Orsino's palace, the Duke has a "man to man" talk with Viola about men's passions, as Viola struggles to keep her own feelings for the Duke secret.

Exit **NARRATOR** *stage rear.*

Enter **DUKE ORSINO, VIOLA,** *and* **CURIO** *from stage left. Enter* **DUKE ORSINO'S BAND** *from stage rear, comically playing over one another.* **DUKE ORSINO** *sits in his throne, with* **VIOLA** *in the chair to his left and* **CURIO** *standing to the right of the table.* **CURIO** *offers an apple slice to* **DUKE ORSINO,** *who takes a thoughtful bite and puts the slice back on the tray. The music stops.*

DUKE ORSINO

> If Music be the food of love, play on!
> Now, good Cesario, but that piece of song,
> That old and antique song we heard last night:
> Methought it did relieve my passion much,
> Come, but one verse.

CURIO

> He is not here, so please your lordship, that should sing it.

CURIO *offers an apple slice to* VIOLA, *who reaches for it then changes her mind. As* CURIO *passes by* BAND, *a member grabs a slice, and the other members roll their eyes. Before she can eat it,* CURIO *snatches the slice away, looks around, cleans it off a bit, and puts it back on the tray. He then takes a bite of fruit himself, and puts the rest in his pocket.*

DUKE ORSINO
> Who was it?

CURIO *(regaining his composure, trying not to reveal that he has eaten the fruit)*
> Feste, the jester, my lord; a fool that the Lady Olivia's father took much delight in: He is about the house.

DUKE ORSINO
> Seek him out: And play the tune the while.

Exit CURIO *stage left.*

Once again, BAND *begins to play, each member playing over the other.*

> Come hither, boy: If ever thou shalt love,
> In the sweet pangs of it remember me;
> How dost thou like this tune?

VIOLA
> It gives a very echo to the seat
> Where Love is throned.

VIOLA *leans against* DUKE ORSINO *while the music plays, and both feel a strange sense of discomfort. The music stops.*

DUKE ORSINO *(regains his composure)*
> Thou dost speak masterly:

My life upon't, young though thou art, thine eye
Hath stay'd upon some favour that it loves;
Hath it not, boy?

VIOLA

A little, by your favour.

DUKE ORSINO

What kind of woman is't?

VIOLA

Of your complexion.

VIOLA *moves her chair closer to his, beginning to lean against him, when they are surprised.*

Enter CURIO *and* FESTE *from stage rear.*

DUKE ORSINO

O, fellow, come, the song we had last night.
It is old and plain,
And dallies with the innocence of love,
Like the old age.

FESTE

Are you ready, sir?

DUKE ORSINO

Ay; prithee, sing.

BAND MEMBER *is about to get her chance for a solo, and there is a silence as she takes time to prepare. She triumphantly blows one note, but is interrupted by a sudden whistle from* FESTE. *Enter* DRUMMERS *stage right, followed by other members of* FESTE'S BAND. ALL *dance and move to the music, with* DUKE ORSINO'S BAND *eventually joining in.*

FESTE *(with singers repeating certain words)*
    Come away, come away, death,
    And in sad cypress let me be laid;
    Fly away, fly away, breath;
    I am slain by a fair cruel maid.
    My shroud of white, stuck all with yew,
    O, prepare it!
    My part of death, no one so true
    Did share it.
    Not a flower, not a flower sweet,
    On my black coffin let there be strown;
    Not a friend, not a friend greet
    My poor corpse, where my bones shall be thrown:
    A thousand thousand sighs to save,
    Lay me, O, where
    Sad true lover never find my grave,
    To weep there!

Exit **FESTE, SINGERS, BANDS,** *and* **CURIO** *stage right, all dancing and drumming.* **DUKE ORSINO** *and* **VIOLA** *look on amusedly. They are alone now.*

VIOLA
    My Lord,
    Say that some lady, as perhaps there is,
    Hath for your love as great a pang of heart
    As you have for Olivia . . .

DUKE ORSINO
    There is no woman's sides
    Can bide the beating of so strong a passion
    As love doth give my heart; no woman's heart
    So big, to hold so much. Make no compare
    Between that love a woman can bear me
    And that I owe Olivia.

(IF PERFORMING MONOLOGUE SOLO, OMIT BRACKETED LINES AND CONTINUE
WITH VIOLA'S SPEECH.)

VIOLA *(to* DUKE ORSINO*)*
>   Ay, but I know—

[**ORSINO**: What dost thou know?]

>   Too well what love women to men may owe.
>   In faith, they are as true of heart as we.
>   My father had a daughter loved a man
>   As it might be, perhaps, were I a woman,
>   I should your Lordship.

[**ORSINO**: And what's her history?]

>   A blank my lord. She never told her love,
>   But let concealment, like a worm i' th' bud,
>   Feed on her damask cheek. She pined in thought,
>   and with a green and yellow melancholy
>   She sat like Patience on a monument,
>   Smiling at grief. Was this not love indeed?
>   We men may say more, swear more, but indeed
>   Our shows are more than will; for still we prove
>   Much in our vows but little in our love.

DUKE ORSINO *(walks sympathetically toward* VIOLA *and puts
his arm around her shoulder)*
>   But died thy sister of her love, my boy?

VIOLA *(liking his touch but also finding it hard to bear; pulls
away, turns, and takes a step forward)*
>   I am all the daughters of my father's house,
>   And all the brothers too; and yet I know not.
>   *(pauses; turns back to him)*
>   Sir, shall I to this lady?

DUKE ORSINO

Ay, that's the theme.

To her in haste; give her this jewel; say,

My love can give no place, bide no delay.

Exit VIOLA *stage right and* DUKE ORSINO *stage rear, both stopping to look back at each other as they leave.*

✳ TWELFTH NIGHT: PERFORMANCE NOTES

Twelfth Night is my favorite Shakespeare play. I love the current of bittersweet longing that runs below the surface of this comedy. The characters of Feste, Maria, Malvolio, Sir Toby Belch, Sir Andrew Aguecheek, Olivia, and Viola are full of charm and depth. The language, the relationships, and the songs paint a theatrical picture that is at once merry and melancholy.

This production was my first outing as a high school play director, in 1997, working under the auspices of the Folger Library, and the only time in my nineteen-year teaching artist residency that I worked with eleventh graders. I was lucky to have a group of students who threw themselves into the project, joyfully occupying some of Shakespeare's richest characters.

The actor who played Feste in this production possessed a natural joy and physical looseness that captivated the audience and garnered him a major award at the Folger Library Secondary School Shakespeare Festival. He moved about the stage with the lilting grace of a basketball player and delivered his lines with a winning grin. Occasionally one has the fortune to encounter someone whose innate charm fills a room. Such was this unforgettable Feste.

As the narrator introduces the roles at the top of the play, each actor crosses the stage in character and exits. This technique offers a fitting preview of the players and sets a merry tone. Sir Toby stumbles onto the bench (with a "fat-pillow" under his shirt), offers his mug to the narrator, who declines, and then falls to the floor. The narrator turns to look at him and then back to the audience, expressionless.

The action gets a laugh and immediately breaks the fourth wall by bringing the narrator into the story as a character. Sir Andrew Aguecheek drags Sir Toby offstage by his feet. Maria dusts the table, and Feste dances a little jig, then hides behind the stage right pillar. Right away the audience sees what kinds of people populate this colorful comedy.

By a stroke of great luck, not only did the student who played Feste overflow with charisma, but he also juggled! On the line, "Those that are fools, let them use their talents," he performed a bit of three-ball juggling with a fancy finish and was met with enthusiastic applause. If your Feste does not juggle, he can balance an ostrich feather, flip a hat onto his head, or do a handstand or somersault. Or he can perform a long build-up to a "nothing trick." Feste's real talent is his wit.

The actor also contributed his own physicalizations. On Feste's line, "God bless you, Lady," he slid on his knees toward Olivia. Raising the physical stakes sheds light on character traits and relationships. Later, when Feste is leaning on the handle of a broom, Malvolio is directed to knock the broom with his cane, causing Feste to fall. In rehearsal Malvolio pushed Feste to the floor instead, and we kept it for the performance. This is a crueler action that casts a small shadow over the light comedy. Importantly, it draws the battle lines between Malvolio and the revelers, which justifies his cruel comeuppance later in the play.

Feste exits the stage in the first scene while bobbing, weaving, and flapping his elbows. He looks like a boxing chicken! Playing "animal essences" is a good way for actors to explore the more primal elements of their characters. The rooster has long been a symbol of the Fool, so Feste's chicken dance is an apt choice—and one that is his own.

We have fun with Viola's attempts to disguise herself as a man. Viola clears her throat before the line "I am a gentleman" in order to speak in a lower pitch. This works best when she first briefly forgets to disguise her high-pitched voice (in the heat of her impassioned speech). By forgetting, then remembering, that she is disguising herself as a man, Viola adds comedy, dramatic tension, and pathos, particularly in her scenes with the Duke.

TWELFTH NIGHT: ACT II, SCENE IV

Sometimes a performer makes a surprising choice. In this production of *Twelfth Night,* the young woman playing the part of Curio decided that her character was gay. There is plenty of cross-dressing and gender bending in the play, and the scenes between both Orsino/Viola and Antonio/Sebastian have distinctly homoerotic overtones. There is nothing in the text to suggest overtly that Curio is gay, but the actress made a strong commitment to her portrayal. The decision informed how she dressed, stood, moved, and even ate an apple.

Curio is a small role, with only two lines in this adaptation. I appreciate how this actor created an inner world for her character that imparted a humanness and dimensionality to the whole scene. Frequently performers believe their smaller roles are unimportant, but this flashy Curio proved otherwise.

The two musicians in this scene, a flute player and a melodica player, provide comic relief. Every time the melodica player tries to play a note, she is interrupted, first by the flute player, then by the drummers, to her increasing frustration. The old adage is true: "There are no small parts, only small actors."

There are three songs in the production, each one distinct and beautiful. "Come Away Death" features a roving rap troupe that enters to accompany Feste, complete with drumming and fist bumps. The call-and-response vocals and unison dance moves bring the energy to a fever pitch, and the piece ends with Feste on his knees across the front of the group, arms akimbo, flashing peace signs with his hands. The audience erupts in sustained applause. This is what it means to "own" a Shakespeare play.

Feste's Song ("Wind and Rain") closed our spirited production of *Twelfth Night*. The entire cast sang the song, with Feste spurring the audience to rhythmic clapping while skipping around the assembled players. The magic of Shakespeare transformed an eleventh grade English class into a troupe of consummate thespians, musicians, comedians, and moving tale-tellers. They provide a rollicking and heartfelt finish to my favorite Shakespeare play; may it touch your heart, too. Using this book as a guideline, I hope the experience of performing this beautiful, bittersweet comedy will bring delight and laughter to actors, educators, and audiences alike.

✳ *TWELFTH NIGHT:* MONOLOGUE NOTES

ACT II, SCENE IV: VIOLA MONOLOGUE

Viola is in love with Orsino, but she cannot demonstrate this to him because she is masquerading as a man. This predicament sets up the comic and dramatic tension for this monologue. Viola and Orsino are discussing traits that they supposedly share as men. But in fact, not only does Viola not share these traits, she is talking about her own love for Orsino in the third person as if it were someone else's. The pull between her affection for Orsino and her inability to express her feelings gives the actor playing Viola ample fodder for dramatic conflict and poignant expression.

Notice the words Viola uses—"true," "heart," "loved"—as they stand in contrast to the darker, sadder images of "blank," "never," "concealment," "pined," "melancholy," "patience," "monument," and "grief." The melancholic words outnumber the loving terms by more than two to one. Each word can be colored with a vocal tone, and some words can also be illustrated with a physical gesture. Even something as small as Viola lowering her eyes and averting them from Orsino can have a large dramatic impact.

During the first part of the speech, in which the "loving" words appear, Viola can approach Orsino and become close to him physically. If playing the monologue as a scene between two performers, the actors can find themselves touching or almost touching, which gives Orsino a chance to experience some confusion at his attraction for Viola.

If the monologue is played solo, Viola can depict this closeness herself and include a moment where she indicates that she and

Orsino are next to one another. This moment could come on the line "I should your Lordship." This line is the only line in the monologue that is not written in iambic pentameter. One can think of the iambic pentameter lines as a heartbeat; when the rhythm is disrupted, perhaps the speaker's heart skips a beat.

Two of Orsino's lines have been left in this monologue. If played solo, the first line, "What dost thou know?" can be eliminated since Viola begins with "Ay, but I know." Viola can speak Orsino's second line herself: "And what's her history?" When doing so, she can pause as if Orsino is looking at her quizzically, and on his behalf, essentially ask the question she thinks his eyes are asking. In this case, the line should be spoken out loud since the phrase "A blank my lord" is the response to the question.

This monologue's mood and performance potential provides an excellent example of the importance of knowing the character's back story. Viola believes she has lost her brother, Sebastian, and although the text does not overtly refer to him, this event has clearly informed her melancholy. Shortly after this monologue, Viola issues a poignant reminder of her loss: "I am all the daughters of my father's house, and all the brothers too."

The actor playing Viola can experiment with using different attitudes when delivering her lines. For example, her final line "We prove much in our vows but little in our love" could be spoken with anger at Orsino. Try substituting the words "you" and "your" for "we" and "our." This exercise will yield an interpretation that might provide the actor with an angrier way to speak the line.

Finally, remember that although the monologue contains much melancholy, it can still be funny. The actor playing Viola can look for places where she might get confused and start acting more like a woman than a man. This is especially true during the initial lines of the monologue when she is discussing her father's daughter's love for Orsino. Perhaps her physical movements and vocal timbre become a little more feminine as she loses herself in her feelings. This gives the actor an opportunity to exploit the inherent comedy in gender confusion. This monologue is bittersweet and poignant but can also leave the audience laughing through their tears.

SUGGESTED VIEWING

TWELFTH NIGHT, 1987
Director: Neil Armfield
Starring: Gillian Jones, Geoffrey Rush

TWELFTH NIGHT, 1996
Director: Trevor Nunn
Starring: Helena Bonham Carter, Imogen Stubbs, Ben Kingsley

✳ THE TWO GENTLEMEN OF VERONA

CHARACTERS IN THE PLAY

The following is a list of characters that appear in this scene of
The Two Gentlemen of Verona.

SILVIA: Beloved of Valentine; daughter to the Duke of Milan
VALENTINE: A gentleman of Verona who woos Silvia
PROTEUS: A gentleman of Verona; in love with Julia, then Silvia
CRAB: a dog
NARRATOR

SET AND PROP LIST

SET PIECES:
Table
Two chairs
Bench
Throne

✳ *THE TWO GENTLEMEN OF VERONA:*
ACT II, SCENE IV

Milan. The Duke's palace.

Enter **NARRATOR** *from stage rear, coming downstage center and leading* **CRAB** *on a leash.*

NARRATOR
> Proteus arrives in Milan and is greeted by his best friend, Valentine, and Valentine's beloved, Silvia. Proteus immediately falls in love with Silvia.

Exit **NARRATOR** *and* **CRAB** *stage left.*

Enter **SILVIA** *and* **VALENTINE** *from stage rear.* **SILVIA** *sits in chair stage right and* **VALENTINE** *sits in chair stage left.*

SILVIA
> Here comes the gentleman.

Enter **PROTEUS** *from stage right.* **VALENTINE** *goes to him, greeting him warmly.*

VALENTINE
> Welcome, dear Proteus!
> Mistress, I beseech you, entertain him
> To be my fellow-servant to your ladyship.

SILVIA
> Too low a mistress for so high a servant.

PROTEUS
>Not so, sweet lady; but too mean a servant
>*(kneels; kisses her hand)*
>To have a look of such a worthy mistress.

VALENTINE *(moves next to* SILVIA*)*
>Leave off discourse of disability:
>Sweet lady, entertain him for your servant.

PROTEUS
>My duty will I boast of, nothing else.

SILVIA
>And duty never yet did want his meed:
>Servant, you are welcome to a worthless mistress.

SILVIA *gestures for* PROTEUS *to sit in stage right chair.*

PROTEUS
>I'll die on him that says so, but yourself.

SILVIA
>That you are welcome?

PROTEUS
>That you are worthless.

VALENTINE *coughs.*

SILVIA
>I'll leave you to confer of home affairs;
>When you have done, I look to hear from you.

PROTEUS
>We'll both attend upon your ladyship.

Exit SILVIA *stage right.*

VALENTINE *walks to Proteus's chair.*

VALENTINE
> Now, tell me, Proteus,
> How does your lady? And how thrives your love?

PROTEUS
> My tales of love were wont to weary you;
> I know you joy not in a love-discourse.

VALENTINE
> Ay, Proteus, but that life is alter'd now.
> *(walks downstage center)*
> For, in revenge of my contempt of love,
> Love hath chased sleep from my enthralled eyes,
> And made them watchers of mine own heart's sorrow.
> O gentle Proteus, Love's a mighty lord,
> And hath so humbled me, as, I confess,
> Now can I break my fast, dine, sup, and sleep,
> Upon the very naked name of love.

PROTEUS *(walks to* VALENTINE*)*
> Enough; I read your fortune in your eye.
> Was this the idol that you worship so?
> *(gestures to where* SILVIA *exited)*

VALENTINE
> Even she; and is she not a heavenly saint?

PROTEUS
> No; but she is an earthly paragon.

VALENTINE
> Call her divine.

PROTEUS

> I will not flatter her.

VALENTINE

> Then speak the truth by her: If not divine,
> Yet let her be a principality,
> Sovereign to all the creatures on the earth.

PROTEUS

> Except my mistress.
> Why, Valentine, what braggardism is this?

VALENTINE

> Pardon me, Proteus: All I can is nothing
> To her, whose worth makes other worthies nothing;
> She is alone.

PROTEUS

> Then let her alone.

VALENTINE

> Not for the world: Why, man, she is mine own;
> And I as rich in having such a jewel
> As twenty seas, if all their sand were pearl,
> The water nectar, and the rocks pure gold.

PROTEUS

> But she loves you?

VALENTINE

> Ay, and we are betroth'd: nay, more, our marriage-
> hour,
> With all the cunning manner of our flight,
> Determined of; how I must climb her window,
> The ladder made of cords; and all the means

Plotted and 'greed on for my happiness.
Good Proteus, go with me to my chamber,
In these affairs to aid me with thy counsel.

PROTEUS

Go on before; I shall inquire you forth:
And then I'll presently attend you.

VALENTINE

Will you make haste?

PROTEUS

I will.

Exit **VALENTINE** *stage right.*

Even as one heat another heat expels,
Or as one nail by strength drives out another,
So the remembrance of my former love
Is by a newer object quite forgotten.
Is it mine eye, or Valentine's praise,
Her true perfection, or my false transgression,
That makes me reasonless to reason thus?
She is fair, and so is Julia that I love—
That I did love, for now my love is thawed,
Which like a waxen image 'gainst a fire
Bears no impression of the thing it was.
Methinks my zeal to Valentine is cold,
And that I love him not as I was wont.
O, but I love his lady too too much,
And that's the reason I love him so little.
How shall I dote on her with more advice
That thus without advice begin to love her?
'Tis but her picture I have yet beheld,
And that hath dazzled my reason's light;
But when I look on her perfections,

There is no reason but I shall be blind.
If I can check my erring love, I will;
If not, to compass her I'll use my skill.

Exit PROTEUS *stage right.*

✴ THE TWO GENTLEMEN OF VERONA: PERFORMANCE NOTES

I directed this performance of *The Two Gentlemen of Verona* in 2001 with a Washington, D.C. public school ninth grade English class.

Courtly music at the top of the play can set the mood for the audience. Lucetta is dusting the furniture. Simple physical motions give us a sense of place and also indicate the occupation and status of the character. This first scene between Julia and her waiting woman Lucetta provides some entertaining nuances regarding status: After Lucetta says, "I do not like this tune," Julia gives her a little pinch.

Lucetta responds by pinching Julia, Julia then slaps Lucetta on the arm, and Lucetta immediately slaps her back. This combative little interchange gets a laugh from the audience. It also serves to illusrate that although Julia is Lucetta's boss, they are on equal footing in many respects. Lucetta is also Julia's friend and confidante, and she is comfortable enough in her relationship to fight with her playfully. Nonetheless, on Julia's line, "Get you gone, and let the papers lie," it remains clear that Julia is the boss.

A good example of levels of physical comedy available to an actor arise in Julia's reading of the ripped pieces of the letter. The letter could be torn into several pieces, not just two. The humor arises from Julia's attempts to put the small pieces of the letter together and from her difficulty reading the tiny segments. When she kisses each individual section of paper, one could become stuck on her tongue, causing her to talk funny. She could accidentally swallow one of the papers, and Lucetta could save her from choking with a Heimlich maneuver. In scenarios like this, exaggerate—and then see if you can exaggerate even more.

Often by going over the top, we surprise the audience into laughter. The play contains broad physical comedy, and it benefits from expansive, exaggerated movements from the actors. The farther you take the physical comedy, by committing to big movements and silliness, the more fun you will have with it, and the audience picks up on the merriment. There is a great range of possibilities and we often don't know what the scope is until we experiment with stretching our limits. This applies not just to vocals, but also to speech combined with movement.

The young man playing the dog in our 2001 production did an admirable job of conveying the clueless loyalty of Crab. He wore a cap with floppy ears and plunked himself by Launce's, staring blankly toward the audience with a faint smile on his face. When Launce removes his shoes for use in the puppet show explanation of his parentage, Crab quickly moves away, as if the shoes have an unpleasant odor to them, a moment the audience enjoys.

We chose to have an actor play the part of Crab, though we could have used a stuffed animal in his place. Generally, a live actor is preferable. The most important element to playing an animal is not to overact, and the actor playing Crab had the proper sense of stillness that made the portrayal complete. Although many comic bits hinge on physical exaggeration, in others, such as with this scene, less is more.

The actor playing Crab cocked his head while curiously attempting to follow Launce's reasoning—and after Launce complained that Crab "speaks not a word," he looked over at Crab, who exclaimed, "Woof!" Exploit the silliness for all its potential laughs. Experiment with the comic possibilities in rehearsal and feel free to free-associate!

THE TWO GENTLEMEN OF VERONA: ACT II, SCENE IV

The narrator enters to describe the scene, accompanied by Crab the Dog on a leash. At the end of her narration, she looks at Crab as if awaiting a translation. Crab says, "Woof." Running gags are a good comedic trick. We repeated this "Woof" a third time. When possible, employ the "rule of three" in comedy. It works!

When Valentine stands to greet Proteus, the two exchange an embrace that suggests a close friendship. When Proteus first lays eyes on Silvia, even before he sits down, there is a pause in which he stops in his tracks and just looks at her. In this way the audience receives foreshadowing of Proteus's attraction to Silvia. Valentine, too, can notice this attraction. When Silvia exits, Valentine occupies the chair where she was sitting and asks Proteus, "How does your lady?" The emphasis is on the word "your," as if Valentine is trying to draw the conversation away from Silvia. These are subtle acting points, but when played with the proper timing and attention to detail, they provide the audience with the subtext necessary to appreciate the nascent conflict between two friends who both admire the same woman.

Both Valentine's and Proteus's speeches in the latter part of the scene contain rich language that must be colored by the actors to achieve their full poetic resonance. The following is a selection of Valentine's words from just four lines of text: "world," "rich," "jewel," "twenty," "seas," "sand," "pearl," "water," "nectar," "rocks," and "gold." And here are some of Proteus's words from his final, amorous speech in the scene: "heat," "nail," "strength," "drives," "remembrance," "former," "love," "newer," "object," "eye," "praise," "true," "perfection," "reasonless," "waxen," "fire," "impression," "erring," "love," "compass," and "skill." Each of these words alone is expressive, and when spoken as part of a line of Shakespeare, they are poetic.

How does one speak "poetically"? The first rule is not to rush. Many actors hurry their lines, which confuses the audience. Writing down beats and breathing points in the script helps curb this problem. Mark a slash in your text at appropriate breathing points. Underline words or syllables that are accentuated, and then experiment with changing the emphasis to hear how this changes a line's meaning.

You can also try "coloring" your words. Think of the word as not just a word, but also something that evokes emotions. See if the word can become a poem in itself, with a richness that echoes its sentiment or enhances the image it arouses. Marking beats and coloring words will encourage you to slow down your speech. Proteus's closing speech, when expressed colorfully, not only advances the plot and conflict, but it also gives the audience a good taste of some of Shakespeare's rich and poetic language.

The play resolves with the promise of two marriages, and all ends well in our Shakespeare comedy. The musicians and cast stand together on the stage, swaying back and forth together in rhythm, clapping and chanting, "One peace, one house, one mutual happiness!"

The students began the process of rehearsing *The Two Gentlemen of Verona* as D.C. public school ninth graders, but by play's end they were Shakespearean actors. May this be your story, too. Using this book as a guideline, I hope that the experience of performing the play will bring delight and laughter to both actors and audiences alike.

✳ *THE TWO GENTLEMEN OF VERONA:* MONOLOGUE NOTES

ACT II, SCENE IV: PROTEUS MONOLOGUE

Proteus is having a debate with himself in this speech. He has fallen instantly in love with Silvia, who is the girlfriend of his best friend Valentine. Proteus is already in love with Julia, so he is understandably conflicted. You can play this scene as a conversation with yourself, or you can choose to speak to the audience. If you are talking with yourself, you will likely make less direct eye contact with audience members. If you are talking to the audience, you can choose specific audience members to look at.

Either choice is valid and has its own advantages and disadvantages. Some speeches lend themselves better to direct audience address because you can use some of your character's traits to bring the audience over to your character's side. An actor performing Iago in *Othello*, for example, will find various ways to use Iago's considerable charm. Try delivering Proteus's speech to yourself and to the audience and decide which works best for you.

Perhaps there is a middle ground. When Proteus asks a question, he could pose it to the audience and then speak to himself the rest of the time. In any monologue, this is one of the decisions an actor makes: Am I talking to myself, to the audience, or to a mix of both?

Proteus begins the speech with a series of three related descriptions or metaphors. The first idea is that one fire drives out another, the second thought is that one nail drives out another, and the third statement is that one love drives out another. He has only moments earlier met and fallen for Julia. This newness should inform how you recite the lines as Proteus. Is he amazed at how quickly Silvia's beauty has forced all thoughts of Julia from his mind? Is he horrified? Are these nail and fire metaphors part of a justification for what he calls his "false transgression"?

Experiment with different approaches to the speech and decide which works for you, remembering that the best choice might be a combination of emotions. For example, when Proteus refers to Julia's "true perfection," his face can reflect how smitten he is with her. He can smile while his eyes can squint as if he is imagining her beauty. Immediately after, when he refers to his "false transgression," his smile can vanish and be replaced with an expression of anguished guilt. Always let the text determine the physical, vocal, and facial decisions that you make as an actor.

Notice that while Proteus never utters Silvia's name, he does say the name of Julia, his "former" love. When he says, "Julia that I love—" he can imbue her name with all the passion he has heretofore felt for her. He can then pause when he realizes that perhaps he does not feel that way about her now that a new beauty has pushed out his old feelings. Perhaps the next line—"That I did love"—can be recited with a cold sobriety that stands in contrast to his former feelings for Julia. Experiment with varying the length of the pause (or beat) before the phrase "That I did love." Proteus's realization that his love for Julia has diminished should be visible in his facial expression. The audience should see the contrast. Videotape yourself or perform in front of a mirror so you can examine the difference between a face that is "in love" and one that "did love." You will see that they are dramatically different faces.

Proteus continues with images of heat and cold, uttering, "for now my love is thawed," as if Silvia's heat has melted whatever shape his love for Julia had. He then concludes that his "zeal to Valentine is cold." How does Proteus feel about that? Valentine is his best friend. At the start of the play, Shakespeare makes their fond feelings for each other clear. In order to give the monologue its true meaning and weight, you have to be familiar with the rest of the play and the relationships. Without knowledge of Proteus's original love for his friend Valentine, it will be difficult to adequately depict his possible distress at falling in love with his best friend's love interest.

At this point, Proteus makes his strongest conclusion: "O, but I love his lady too too much, and that's the reason I love him so little." This moment of certainty does not last long, though, as he continues to ask himself another question: "How shall I dote on her with more advice/That thus without advice begin to love her?" Notice the rhythm in these two lines. The first ("How shall I dote on her with more advice") is written in iambic pentameter. The second ("That thus without advice begin to love her?") has one extra syllable with the word "her." Recite that sequence out loud. Do you hear how the word "her" naturally hangs in the air at the end of the line? Pause before saying it and then infuse "her" with all the newfound passion that Proteus has for Silvia. Use the natural rhythm of the lines, and variations in rhythm, to your advantage.

Proteus continues to go back and forth between feeling "dazzled" by Silvia's image (her "picture") and smitten by her "perfections." That is, he knows that his love is "blind" and "erring" but concludes with the decision that if he can "check" his love, then "to compass her I'll use my skill." The conflict of the entire monologue is neatly encapsulated in this last couplet. For the first line ("If I can check my erring love, I will"), try summoning up Proteus's conscience and sense of duty to his friend. Square your shoulders and stiffen your spine. Then on the final line ("If not, to compass her I'll use my skill"), show the audience the other side to Proteus, the love-hunter!

As the speech ends, Proteus no longer questions his love for Silvia. A new Proteus has emerged: a young man who will stop at nothing to win the love of a new woman, even if it means losing a best friend and former lover in the process.

This monologue serves as an example of the importance of knowing the character's speech in the context of the whole play. By studying Proteus's existing relationship with Valentine and Julia in earlier scenes, you will become more adept at expressing his conflict in this monologue. The more an actor examines the play itself, the better he will be able to portray his character in an individual scene by bringing breadth and emotion to Shakespeare's words.

SUGGESTED VIEWING

THE TWO GENTLEMEN OF VERONA, 1952
Director: Denis Carey
Starring: John Neville, Pamela Alan

THE TWO GENTLEMEN OF VERONA, 1983
Director: Don Taylor
Starring: Tyler Butterworth, John Hudson, Tessa Peake-Jones

✳ PERFORMING SHAKESPEARE

HOW *THE 30-MINUTE SHAKESPEARE* WAS BORN

In 1981 I performed a "Shakespeare Juggling" piece called "To Juggle or Not To Juggle" at the first Folger Library Secondary School Shakespeare Festival. The audience consisted of about 200 Washington, D.C. area high school students who had just performed thirty-minute versions of Shakespeare plays for each other and were jubilant over the experience. I was dressed in a jester's outfit, and my job was to entertain them. I juggled and jested and played with Shakespeare's words, notably Hamlet's "To be or not to be" soliloquy, to very enthusiastic response. I was struck by how much my "Shakespeare Juggling" resonated with a group who had just performed Shakespeare themselves. "Getting" Shakespeare is a heady feeling, and I am continually delighted at how much joy and satisfaction young people derive from performing Shakespeare. Simply reading and studying this great playwright does not even come close to inspiring the kind of enthusiasm that comes from performance.

Surprisingly, many of these students were not "actor types." A good percentage of the students performing Shakespeare that day were part of an English class that had rehearsed the plays during class time. Fifteen years later, when I first started directing plays in D.C. public schools as a teaching artist with the Folger Shakespeare Library's wonderful education department, I entered a ninth grade English class as a guest and spent two or three days a week for two or three months preparing students for the Folger's annual Secondary School Shakespeare Festival. I have conducted this annual residency with Folger ever since. Every year for seven action-packed days, eight groups of students between grades seven and twelve tread the boards at the Folger's Elizabethan Theatre, a grand recreation of a sixteenth-century venue with a three-tiered gallery, carved oak columns, and a sky-painted canopy.

As noted on the Folger website (www.folger.edu), "The festival is a celebration of the Bard, not a competition. Festival commentators—drawn from the professional theater and Shakespeare education communities—recognize exceptional performances, student directors, and good spirit amongst the students with selected awards at the end of each day. They are also available to share feedback with the students."

My annual Folger teaching artist engagement, directing a Shakespeare play in a public high school English class, is the most challenging and the most rewarding thing I do all year. I hope this book can bring you the same rewards.

GETTING STARTED: GAMES

How can you start the seemingly daunting task of performing a Shakespeare play? You have already successfully completed the critical first step, which is buying this book. You hold in your hand eighteen performance-ready Shakespeare scenes and monologues, with stage directions and detailed monologue notes to help you move about the stage purposefully, and to speak the language beautifully. But it's a good idea to get warmed up with some theater games.

One good initial exercise is called "Positive/Negative Salutations." Actors stand in two lines facing each other (four or five students in each line) and, reading from index cards, greet each other, first with a "Positive" salutation in Shakespeare's language (using actual phrases from the plays), followed by a "negative" greeting.

Additionally, short vocal exercises are an essential part of the preparation process. The following is a very simple and effective vocal warm-up: Beginning with the number two, have the whole group count to twenty using increments of two (i.e., "Two, four, six . . ."). Increase the volume slightly with each number, reaching top volume with "twenty," and then decrease the volume while counting back down, so that you are practically whispering when you arrive again at "two." This exercise teaches dynamics and allows you to get loud as a group without any individual pressure. Frequently during a rehearsal period, if an actor is mumbling inaudibly, I will refer back to this exercise as a reminder that we can, and often do, belt it out!

"Stomping Words" is a game that is very helpful at getting a handle on Shakespeare's rhythm. Choose a passage in iambic pentameter and walk around the room in a circle, stomping your feet on the second beat of each line:

> Two **house**-holds, **both** a-**like** in **dig**-nity
> In fair Ve-**rona** **Where** we **lay** our **scene**

Do the same thing with a prose passage, discuss with the group your experience with it, including points at which there is an extra beat, etc., and what, if anything, it might signify.

I end every vocal warm-up with a group reading of one of the speeches from the play, emphasizing diction and projection, bouncing off consonants, and encouraging the group members to listen to each other so that they can speak the lines together in unison. For variety I will throw in some classic tongue twisters, too, such as, "The sixth sheik's sixth sheep is sick."

The Folger Shakespeare Library's website (www.folger.edu) and their book series *Shakespeare Set Free,* edited by Peggy O'Brien, are two great resources for getting started with a performance-based teaching of Shakespeare in the classroom. The Folger website has numerous helpful resources and activities, many submitted by teachers, for helping a class actively participate in the process of getting to know a Shakespeare play. For more simple theater games, Viola Spolin's *Theatre Games for the Classroom* is very helpful, as is one I use frequently, *Theatre Games for Young Performers.*

HATS AND PROPS

Introducing a few hats and props early in the process is a good way to get the action going. Hats, in particular, provide a nice avenue for giving you a non-verbal way of getting into character. In the opening weeks, when players are still holding onto their scripts, a hat can give an actor a way to "feel" like a character. You are already a natural masters at injecting your own personality into what you wear, and even small choices made with how a hat is worn (jauntily, shadily, cockily, mysteriously) provide a starting point for discussion of specific characters, their traits, and their relationships with other characters. All such discussions always lead back to one thing: the text. "Mining the text" is consistently the best strategy for uncovering the mystery of Shakespeare's language. That is where all the answers lie: in the words themselves.

WHAT DO THE WORDS MEAN?

It is essential that you know what you are saying when you recite Shakespeare. If not, you might as well be scat singing, riffing on sounds and rhythm but not conveying a specific meaning. The real question is: What do the words mean? The answer is multifaceted, and can be found in more than one place. The New Folger Library paperback editions of the plays themselves (edited by Barbara Mowat and Paul Werstine, Washington Square Press) are a great resource for understanding Shakespeare's words and passages and "translating" them into modern English. These editions also contain chapters on Shakespeare's language, his life, his theater, a "Modern Perspective," and further reading. There is a wealth of scholarship embedded in these wonderful books, and I make it a point to read them cover to cover before embarking on a play-directing project. At the very least, go through the explanatory notes that appear on the pages facing the text. These explanatory notes are an indispensable "translation tool."

The best way to understand what Shakespeare's words mean is to ask yourself what you think they mean. You have your own associations with the words and with how they sound and feel. The best ideas on how to perform Shakespeare often come directly from your own interpretation, not from anybody else's notion. If an actor has an idea or feeling about a word or passage, and it resonates with her emotionally, physically, or spiritually, then Shakespeare's words can be a vehicle for her feelings. That can result in some powerful performances!

I make it my job as director to read the explanatory notes in the Folger text, but I make it clear to the students that almost "anything goes" when trying to understand Shakespeare. There are no wrong interpretations. Actors have their own experiences, with some shared and some uniquely their own. If someone has an association with the phrase "canker-blossom," or if the words make that performer or his character feel or act a certain way, then that is the "right" way to decipher it.

I encourage you to refer to the Folger text's explanatory notes and to keep a pocket dictionary handy. You must attach some meaning to every word or line they recite. If I feel an actor is glossing over a word, I will stop him and ask him what he is saying. If he doesn't know, we will figure it out together as a group.

PROCESS VS. PRODUCT

The process of learning Shakespeare by performing one of his plays is more important than whether everybody remembers his lines or whether somebody misses a cue or an entrance. But my teaching artist residencies have always had the end goal of a public performance for about 200 other students, so naturally the performance starts to take precedence over the process somewhere around dress rehearsal. It is your job to be prepared. It takes work to earn the glorious triumph of owning a Shakespeare play.

In one of my earlier years of play directing, I was sitting in the audience as one of my narrators stood frozen on stage for at least a minute, trying to remember her opening line. I started scrambling in my backpack below my seat for a script, at last prompting her from the audience. Despite her fine performance, that embarrassing moment is all she remembered from the whole experience. Since then I have made sure to assign at least one person to prompt from backstage if necessary. Additionally, I inform the entire cast that if somebody is dying alone out there, it is okay to rescue him or her with an offstage prompt.

There is always a certain amount of stage fright that will accompany a performance, especially a public one for an unfamiliar audience. As a director, I live with stage fright as well, even though I am not appearing on stage. The only antidote to this is work and preparation. If you are struggling with your lines, run lines with a friend or family member in person or over the telephone. I try to set up a buddy system so that students can run lines with their peers, and this often works well. But if somebody does not have a "buddy," I will personally make the time to help out myself. Help each other out!

It is a good idea to culminate in a public performance, as opposed to an in-class project, even if it is only for another classroom. Actors want to show their Shakespearian thespian skills to an outside group, and this goal motivates them to do a good job. In that respect, "product" is important. Another wonderful bonus to performing a play is that it is a unifying group effort. Actors learn teamwork. They learn to give focus to another actor when he is speaking, and to play off of other characters. I like to end each performance with the entire cast reciting a passage in unison. This is a powerful ending, one that reaffirms the unity of the group.

SEEING SHAKESPEARE PERFORMED

It is very helpful to see Shakespeare performed by a group of professionals, whether they are appearing live on stage (preferable but not always possible) or on film. There is also the Internet, specifically YouTube. A quick YouTube search for "Shakespeare" can unearth thousands of results, many appropriate for the classroom.

The first "Hamlet" result showed an 18-year-old African American actor on the streets of Camden, New Jersey, delivering a riveting performance of Hamlet's "The play's the thing." The second clip was from *Cat Head Theatre*, an animation of cats performing Hamlet. Of course, YouTube boasts not just alley cats and feline thespians, but also clips by true legends of the stage, such as John Gielgud and Richard Burton. These clips can provide useful inspiration.

One advantage of the amazing variety of clips available on YouTube is that you can witness the wide range of interpretations for any given scene, speech, or character in Shakespeare, thus freeing you from any preconceived notion that there is a "right" way to do it. Furthermore, modern interpretations of the Bard may appeal to those who are put off by the "thees and thous" of Elizabethan speech.

By seeing Shakespeare performed either live or on film, actors are able to hear the cadence, rhythm, vocal dynamics, and pronunciation of the language, and they can appreciate the life that other performers breathe into the characters. They get to see the story told dramatically, which inspires them to tell their own version.

GET OUTSIDE HELP

Every time there is a fight scene in one of the plays I am directing, I call on my friend Michael Tolaydo, a professional actor and theater professor at St. Mary's College, who is an expert in all aspects of theater, including fight choreography. Not only does Michael stage the fight, but he does so in a way that furthers the action of the play, highlighting character's traits and bringing out the best in the student actors. Fight choreography must be done by an expert or somebody could get hurt. In the absence of such help, super slow-motion fights are always a safe bet and can be quite effective, especially when accompanied by a soundtrack on the boom box.

During dress rehearsals I invite my friend Hilary Kacser, a Washington-area actor and dialect coach for two decades. Because I bring her in late in the rehearsal process, I have her direct her comments to me, which I then filter and relay to the cast. This avoids confusing the cast with a second set of directions. This caveat only applies to general directorial comments from outside visitors. Comments on specific artistic disciplines such as dance, music, and stage combat can come from the outside experts themselves.

If you are in a school, you might have helpful resources within your own building, such as a music or dance teacher who could contribute their expertise to a scene. If nobody is available in your school, try seeking out a member of the local professional theater. Many local performing artists will be glad to help, and students are usually thrilled to have a visit from a professional performer.

BRING YOURSELF INTO THE PLAY

The best ideas often come from the actors themselves. If an actor has a notion of how to play a scene, I will always give that idea a try. In a rehearsal of *Henry IV, Part 1*, one traveler jumped into the other's arms when they were robbed. It got a huge laugh. This was something that they did on instinct. We kept that bit for the performance, and it worked wonderfully.

You have to feel safe to experiment. In the same production of *Henry IV*, Falstaff and Hal invented a little fist bump "secret handshake" to use in the battle scene. The actors were having fun and bringing parts of themselves into the play. Shakespeare himself would have approved. When possible I try to err on the side of fun because if performers are having fun, then they will commit themselves to the project. The beauty of the language, the story, the characters, and the pathos will follow.

There is a balance to be achieved here, however. In that same production of *Henry IV, Part 1*, the actor who played Bardolph was having a great time with her character. She carried a leather wineskin around and offered it up to the other characters in the tavern. It was a prop with which she developed a comic relationship. At the end of our thirty-minute *Henry IV, Part 1*, I added a scene from *Henry IV, Part 2* as a coda: The new King Henry V (formerly Falstaff's drinking and carousing buddy Hal) rejects Falstaff, banishing him from within ten miles of the King. It is a sad and sobering moment, one of the most powerful in the play.

But at the performance, in the middle of the King's rejection speech (played by a female student, and her only speech), Bardolph offered her flask to King Henry and got a big laugh, thus not only upstaging the King but also undermining the seriousness and poignancy of the whole scene. She did not know any better; she was bringing herself to the character as I had been encouraging her to do. But it was inappropriate, and in subsequent seasons, if I foresaw something like that happening as an individual joyfully occupied a character, I attempted to prevent it. Some things we cannot predict. Now I make sure to issue a statement warning against changing any of the blocking on show day, and to watch out for upstaging one's peers.

FOUR FORMS OF ENGAGEMENT: VOCAL, EMOTIONAL, PHYSICAL, AND INTELLECTUAL

When studying a Shakespeare play for performance, always start with the words themselves because the words have the power to engage the emotions, mind, and body. The words have the power to trigger a switch in both the teller and the listener, eliciting both an emotional and physical reaction. I have never heard a student utter the line "Fie! Fie! You counterfeit, you puppet you!" without seeing him change before my eyes. His spine stiffens, his eyes widen, and his fingers point menacingly.

Having used Shakespeare's words to engage you emotionally and physically, you can then return to the text for a more reflective discussion of what the words mean to you personally. Understand intellectually what they feel like viscerally. The advantage to a performance-based teaching of Shakespeare is that by engaging yourself vocally, emotionally, and physically, it is then much easier to engage yourself intellectually because you are invested in the words, the characters, and the story.

SIX ELEMENTS OF DRAMA: PLOT, CHARACTER, THEME, DICTION, MUSIC, AND SPECTACLE

Over two thousand years ago, Aristotle's *Poetics* outlined six elements of drama, in order of importance: Plot, Character, Theme, Diction, Music, and Spectacle. Because Shakespeare was foremost a playwright, it is helpful to take a brief look at these six elements as they relate to directing a Shakespeare play in the classroom.

PLOT (ACTION)

To Aristotle, plot was the most important element. For the sake of a full understanding of the characters' relationships and motivations, it is helpful to make short plot summaries of each scene so that you are aware of their characters' arcs throughout the play. The scene descriptions in the Folger editions are sufficient to fill in the plot holes. Make sure the story is clear to you, and that no plot elements are neglected. Additionally, there are one-page charts in the Folger editions of *Shakespeare Set Free*, indicating characters' relations graphically, with lines connecting families and factions to give students a visual representation of what can often be complex interrelationships, particularly in Shakespeare's history plays.

Actors love action. That is why *The 30-Minute Shakespeare* includes dynamic blocking (stage direction) that allows performers to tell the story in a physically dramatic fashion. Characters' movements on the stage are always motivated by the text itself.

CHARACTER

Your understanding of the characters should spring from the text and the story. From there, I encourage you to consider how your character might talk, walk, stand, sit, eat, and drink. Consider characters' motivations, objectives, and relationships, and ask pointed questions to that end during the rehearsal process. Always make sure to leave room to bring yourself into the character because your own ideas are invariably the best.

THEME (THOUGHTS, IDEAS)

Using a performance-based method of teaching Shakespeare, an understanding of the play's themes develops from "mining the text" and exploring Shakespeare's words and his story. If you understand what you are saying and how that relates to your character and the overall story, the plays' themes will emerge clearly. Always return to the text itself. There are a number of elegant computer programs, such as www.wordle.net, that will count the number of recurring words in a passage and illustrate them graphically. For example, if the word "jealousy" comes up more than any other word in *Othello*, it will appear in a larger font. Seeing the words displayed by size in this way can offer up illuminating insights into the interaction between words in the text and the play's themes. Computer-minded students might enjoy searching for such tidbits. There are more internet tools and websites in the *Additional Resources* section at the back of this book.

I cannot overstress the importance of acting out the play in understanding its themes. By embodying the roles of Othello and Iago and reciting their words, actors do not simply comprehend the themes intellectually, but understand them kinesthetically, physically, and emotionally. They are essentially **living** the characters' jealousy, pride, and feelings about race. The themes of appearance versus reality, good versus evil, honesty, misrepresentation, and self-knowledge (or lack thereof) become physically felt as well as intellectually understood. Performing Shakespeare delivers a richer understanding than that which comes from just reading the play. Performers can now relate the characters' conflicts to their own struggles.

DICTION (LANGUAGE)

If I had to cite one thing I would like my actors to take from their experience of performing a play by William Shakespeare, it is an appreciation and understanding of the beauty of Shakespeare's language. The language is where it all begins and ends. Shakespeare's stories are dramatic, his characters are rich and complex, and his settings are exotic and fascinating, but it is through his language that these all achieve their richness. This leads me to spend more time on language than on any other element of the performance.

Starting with daily vocal warm-ups, many of them using parts of the script or other Shakespearean passages, I consistently emphasize the importance of the words. In addition to comprehension, I emphasize projection, diction, breathing, pacing, dynamics, coloring of words, and vocal energy. *Theatre Games for Young Performers* contains many effective vocal exercises, as does the Folger's *Shakespeare Set Free* series. Consistent emphasis on all aspects of Shakespeare's language, especially on how to speak it effectively, is the most important element to any Shakespeare performance.

MUSIC

A little music can go a long way in setting a mood for a Shakespeare performance. I usually open the show with a short passage of music to set the tone. Thirty seconds of music played on a boom box can provide a nice introduction to the play, create an atmosphere for the audience, and give the actors a sense of place and feeling.

iTunes is a good starting point for choosing your music. Typing in "Shakespeare" or "Hamlet" or "jealousy" (if you are going for a theme) will result in an excellent selection of aural performance enhancers at the very reasonable price of ninety-nine cents each (or free of charge; see *Additional Resources* section.) Likewise, fight sounds, foreboding sounds, weather sounds (rain, thunder), trumpet sounds, etc. are all readily available online at affordable cost. I typically include three sound cues in a play, just enough to enhance but not overpower a production.

SPECTACLE

Aristotle considered spectacle the least important aspect of drama. People tend to be surprised at this since we are used to being bombarded with production values on TV and video, often at the expense of substance. In my early days of putting on student productions, I would find myself hamstrung by my own ambitions in the realm of scenic design.

A simple bench or two chairs set on the stage are sufficient. The sense of "place" can be achieved through language and acting. Simple set dressing, a few key props, and some tasteful, emblematic costume pieces will go a long way toward providing all the "spectacle" you need.

Take a good look at the performing space you will be using and see if there are any elements that can be incorporated into your own stage directions. Is there a balcony? Can characters enter from the audience? (Make sure that they can get there from backstage, unless you want them waiting in the lobby until their entrance, which may be impractical.) If possible, make sure to rehearse in that space a few times to fix any technical issues and perhaps discover a few fun staging variations that will add pizzazz and dynamics to your own show.

The real spectacle is in the telling of the tale. Wooden swords are handy for characters that need them. Playing with swords outside of the scene is verboten. Letters, moneybags, and handkerchiefs should all have plentiful duplicates kept in a small prop box, as well as with a stage manager, because they tend to disappear. After every rehearsal and performance, I recommend you personally sweep the rehearsal or performance area immediately for stray props. It is amazing what gets left behind.

Ultimately, the performances are about language and human drama, not set pieces, props, and special effects. Fake blood, glitter, glass, and liquids can be a recipe for disaster, or, at the very least, a big mess. On the other hand, the props that are employed can often be used effectively to convey character, as in Bardolph's aforementioned relationship with his wineskin.

PITFALLS AND SOLUTIONS

Performing a play, a scene, or a monologue is not easy. There are problems with enthusiasm, attitude, attention, and line memorization, to name a few. It is always darkest before the dawn. My experience is that after one or two days of utter despair just before the play goes up, show day breaks and the play miraculously shines. To quote a recurring gag in one of my favorite movies, *Shakespeare in Love:* "It's a mystery."

ENTHUSIASM, FRUSTRATION, AND DISCIPLINE

Bring the enthusiasm yourself. Feed on the energy of positive people, and others will pick up on that. Keep focused on the task at hand. Arrive prepared. Enthusiasm comes as you make headway. Ultimately, it helps to remember that a "play" is fun. I try to focus on the positive aspects of the experience, rather than the ones that drive me crazy.

LINE MEMORIZATION

Actors may have a hard time memorizing lines. In these cases, see if you can get paired up with a "buddy" or existing friend who will run lines with you in person or over the phone after school.

If serious line memorization problems arise that cannot be solved through work, then two students can switch parts if it is early enough in the rehearsal process. For doubled roles, the scene with fewer lines can go to the actor who is having memorization problems. Additionally, a few passages or lines can be cut. Again, it is important to address these issues early. Later cuts become more problematic as other actors have already memorized their cues. I have had to do late cuts about twice in nineteen years. While they have gotten us out of jams, it is best to assess early whether a student will have line memorization problems, and deal with the problem sooner rather than later.

In production, always keep several copies of the script backstage, as well as cheat sheets indicating cues, entrances, and scene changes. Make a prop list, indicating props for each scene, as well as props that are the responsibility of individual actors. Direct the stage manager and an assistant stage manager to keep track of these items, and on show days, personally double-check if you can.

In nineteen years of preparing an inner-city public high school English class for a public performance on a field trip to the Folger Secondary School Shakespeare Festival, my groups and I have been beset by illness, emotional turmoil, discipline problems, stage fright, adolescent angst, midlife crises (not theirs), and all manner of other emergencies, including acts of God and nature. Despite the difficulties and challenges inherent in putting on a Shakespeare play with a group of young actors, one amazing fact stands out in my experience. Here is how many times a performer has been absent for show day: Zero. Somehow, everybody has always made it to the show, and the show has gone on. How can this be? It's a mystery.

ADDITIONAL RESOURCES

SHAKESPEARE

Shakespeare Set Free: Teaching Romeo and Juliet, Macbeth and a Midsummer Night's Dream
Peggy O'Brien, Ed., Teaching Shakespeare Institute
Washington Square Press
New York, 1993

Shakespeare Set Free: Teaching Hamlet and Henry IV, Part 1
Peggy O'Brien, Ed., Teaching Shakespeare Institute
Washington Square Press
New York, 1994

Shakespeare Set Free: Teaching Twelfth Night and Othello
Peggy O'Brien, Ed., Teaching Shakespeare Institute
Washington Square Press
New York, 1995

The *Shakespeare Set Free* series is an invaluable resource with lesson plans, activites, handouts, and excellent suggestions for rehearsing and performing Shakespeare plays in a classroom setting.

ShakesFear and How to Cure It!
Ralph Alan Cohen
Prestwick House, Inc.
Delaware, 2006

The Friendly Shakespeare:
A Thoroughly Painless Guide
to the Best of the Bard
Norrie Epstein
Penguin Books
New York, 1994

Brush Up Your Shakespeare!
Michael Macrone
Cader Books
New York, 1990

Shakespeare's Insults:
Educating Your Wit
Wayne F. Hill and Cynthia J. Ottchen
Three Rivers Press
New York, 1991

Practical Approaches to
Teaching Shakespeare
Peter Reynolds
Oxford University Press
New York, 1991

Scenes From Shakespeare:
A Workbook for Actors
Robin J. Holt
McFarland and Co.
London, 1988

THEATER AND PERFORMANCE

Impro: Improvisation and the Theatre
Keith Johnstone
Routledge Books
London, 1982

A Dictionary of Theatre Anthropology:
The Secret Art of the Performer
Eugenio Barba and Nicola Savarese
Routledge
London, 1991

THEATER GAMES

Theatre Games for Young Performers
Maria C. Novelly
Meriwether Publishing
Colorado, 1990

Improvisation for the Theater
Viola Spolin
Northwestern University Press
Illinois, 1983

Theater Games for Rehearsal:
A Director's Handbook
Viola Spolin
Northwestern University Press
Illinois, 1985

101 Theatre Games for Drama
Teachers, Classroom Teachers
& Directors
Mila Johansen
Players Press Inc.
California, 1994

PLAY DIRECTING

Theater and the Adolescent Actor:
Building a Successful School Program
Camille L. Poisson
Archon Books
Connecticut, 1994

Directing for the Theatre
W. David Sievers
Wm. C. Brown, Co.
Iowa, 1965

The Director's Vision: Play Direction
from Analysis to Production
Louis E. Catron
Mayfield Publishing Co.
California, 1989

INTERNET RESOURCES

http://www.folger.edu
The Folger Shakespeare Library's
website has lesson plans, primary
sources, study guides, images,
workshops, programs for teachers
and students, and much more. The
definitive Shakespeare website for
educators, historians and all lovers
of the Bard.

http://www.shakespeare.mit.edu.
The Complete Works of
William Shakespeare.
All complete scripts for *The 30-Minute Shakespeare* series were originally downloaded from this site before editing. Links to other internet resources.

http://www.LoMonico.com/
Shakespeare-and-Media.htm
http://shakespeare-and-media
.wikispaces.com
Michael LoMonico is Senior Consultant on National Education for the Folger Shakespeare Library. His *Seminar Shakespeare 2.0* offers a wealth of information on how to use exciting new approaches and online resources for teaching Shakespeare.

http://www.freesound.org.
A collaborative database of sounds and sound effects.

http://www.wordle.net.
A program for creating "word clouds" from the text that you provide. The clouds give greater prominence to words that appear more frequently in the source text.

http://www.opensourceshakespeare
.org.
This site has good searching capacity.

http://shakespeare.palomar.edu/
default.htm
Excellent links and searches

http://shakespeare.com/
Write like Shakespeare,
Poetry Machine, tag cloud

http://www.shakespeare-online.com/

http://www.bardweb.net/

http://www.rhymezone.com/
shakespeare/
Good searchable word and phrase finder.
Or by lines:
http://www.rhymezone.com/
shakespeare/toplines/

http://shakespeare.mcgill.ca/
Shakespeare and Performance research team

http://www.enotes.com/william-
shakespeare

Needless to say, the internet goes on and on with valuable Shakespeare resources. The ones listed here are excellent starting points and will set you on your way in the great adventure that is Shakespeare.

NICK NEWLIN has been performing the comedy and variety act Nicolo Whimsey for over 30 years. Since 1996, he has conducted an annual teaching artist residency with the Folger Shakespeare Library in Washington, D.C. Newlin received a BA with Honors from Harvard University in 1982, and an MA in Theater with an emphasis in Play Directing from the University of Maryland in 1996.

THE 30-MINUTE
SHAKESPEARE

All titles approximately 72 pages, $7.95, print and ebook editions available at bookstores everywhere

CPSIA information can be obtained at www.ICGtesting.com
Printed in the USA
LVOW11s0836250416

485179LV00001B/2/P